Leadership Lessons
from the Age of
Fighting Sail

NEW YORK TIMES BESTSELLING AUTHOR
CHRIS BRADY

First Edition, December 2014
10 9 8 7 6 5 4 3 2 1

Published by:

Obstaclés Press
200 Commonwealth Court
Cary, NC 27511

Scripture quotations marked "KJV" are taken from the Holy Bible, King James Version, Cambridge, 1769.

chrisbrady.com

ISBN: 978-0-9909619-1-8

Cover design and layout by Norm Williams, nwa-inc.com

Printed in the United States of America

In memory of Jackie Lewis

"Bring me that horizon!"
—Captain Jack Sparrow in the movie *Pirates of the Caribbean: The Curse of the Black Pearl*

CONTENTS

PREFACE

You're cold. The salty wind bites right through your thick wool coat and even finds its way past your waistcoat. You hold your hat firmly to your head and squint at the gray horizon, thinking that your eyes aren't as sharp as they used to be. The deck pitches beneath you, but you barely notice. And your ears picking up the sound of the wind in the rigging subconsciously tell you that everything is trimmed just as you like. The ship, the sails, the weapons below deck, the wind, the waves, navigation, stores—they're all part of your natural environment. It's all a matter of course for you. You manage them all with the cool proficiency that comes only with years of experience.

You know, however, that there is way more to victory than proficient management. You know this well. As you stare at the bodies swarming up the ratlines and around the myriad of obstacles on deck, you think of the crew. It's the men, and the leadership they follow, who make all the difference. As if on cue with your thoughts, one of them breaks the silence and stands at attention in front of you, rain dripping from his whiskers. "Orders, sir?"

You are in command. Your job is so challenging, so complex, so never-ending that most people could never come close to understanding the load you carry. You are thrust into impossible situations with little time and usually even less information upon which to make a decision. And you are entirely responsible for the outcomes, good or bad. You will be subject to critical analysis and scrutiny from people not engaged in the heat of the moment, not under the pressure of responsibility, and not in your boots. They will pick you apart and be quick to judge every little thing you do. But that's leadership, you think. It's what you love.

"Orders, sir?" the man repeats, and you detect a measure of impatience or panic in his voice. He needs your decision, and he needs it now. Everyone aboard is waiting for it, counting on it, depending on it to be right. And as always, there is no time to lose.

You make your choice and pray that it's right. Then you do everything in your power to *make* it right, knowing there is no turning back. In sum, you do what is expected of you—indeed, what you expect from yourself: you lead!

INTRODUCTION

It was perhaps the most unusual navy ever seen. Built from green wood hastily chopped in the dense forests of New York, it included one sloop, three schooners, eight gondolas, and five galleys and was manned almost entirely by landsmen. Its very construction by the crafty American colonials had forced the building of an opposing fleet by the British of Canada. This program alone delayed the British plan to invade the upstart colonies from the north along the navigable lakes of Champlain and George. The ensuing battle would cost even more time.

The commander of the colonial fleet was Benedict Arnold. Although his name would later be remembered for other matters, on that day near Valcour Island, he led his fleet to a tactical victory. Even though most of his ships were annihilated, Arnold was successful in forcing the British back to the north for the winter and thereby delaying their invasion for an entire season. It was this delay that set the stage for the surprising upset of the flamboyant British general Burgoyne at Saratoga the following year. In turn, the colonial victory at Saratoga was what convinced the French crown to throw its mighty influence, wealth, and arms into the American cause. The help from the French would be the turning point of the War for Independence.

Benedict Arnold at Valcour Island is an excellent illustration of the effect one leader can have on events. Facing incredible odds, outnumbered, outgunned, and with a crew lacking experience to match its foe, Arnold was still able to lead his men in a heroic stand that had global ramifications. But there is more to the story, as there usually is. Arnold was also wracked with political strife within his command structure in the colonial army. Rivals were undercutting him at nearly every turn. He was not good at politics. He was hot-tempered and vain. His men, however, loved him. Arnold was brave and led from the front. He commanded respect because he got results. He broke the rules when necessary and showed incredible ingenuity and creativity where obvious solutions were lacking. In short, he was an imperfect man in a flawed organization facing losing odds.

To any leader in today's world, this should sound familiar. Rising above these challenges and accomplishing something great in spite of the facts is what leadership is really all about. It just seems clearer when it is demonstrated in living color by a real person in a real challenge. That is the reason for this book.

Leadership is influencing others in a productive, vision-driven direction. It is done through the character, conviction, and example of the leader. Leadership is both science and art. Much of it can be taught, but the rest must be "caught." Although anyone can learn the fundamentals of leadership principles, what separates the good leaders from the great is the art side of the formula. In other words, effective leadership always involves more than a paint-by-numbers or dot-to-dot connection of precepts and platitudes. Unfortunately, most of what claims to be leadership training in the marketplace today is little more than instruction in the science side: the how-tos, the details, the lists of principles to be followed. Mastering this portion of the field of leadership is certainly important but can only take one so far.

What really needs to be mastered is the art side of leadership. This is the component of leadership that is difficult to describe, but, like Arnold at Valcour Island, we know it when we see it. Adding spice to the mix is the fact that art, arguably, cannot be captured in full. Most artists would say their work could never reach its zenith. A painting could always be better; a book could always use a little more tweaking (this one not excepted!). So it is with leadership. Whether one is just beginning a journey of leadership or has a lifetime of experience in the influence of others, there is always more to learn. A leader can always increase his or her effectiveness.

How, then, is an art such as leadership to be mastered?

Certainly, experience is a large ingredient, although unexamined experience provides no advancement. Thirty years of experience at something, if not properly comprehended and applied, could result in no more than the equivalent of one year's experience repeated thirty times. Experience must be sifted and understood in order to glean its lessons and receive its full value. Learning from experience and changing behavior accordingly is one possible definition of wisdom.

Additionally though, the experience of *others* becomes invaluable. It acts as a shortcut to bypass the long and painful process of trial and error. Indeed, all wise leaders learn from others, both contemporary and historical. One common and effective admonishment for leaders is to identify an objective, find someone who successfully accomplished a similar objective, learn how that person did it, and do what he or she did.

Even this, however, doesn't go far enough to produce mastery. What really needs to be learned from other successful leaders is their thought processes, their reasons, their methods of emotional control, their strategies, their abilities in dealing with other people, their subtle touches.

It is in these areas where the art side of leadership gets its play. It is in the subtleties and the sublime that art truly flourishes. In order to learn from the leadership of others, we might be served best by accessing a theatre of operations rich in situations that showcase these important aspects of the craft. We can discuss art all we want, but to truly comprehend it, we must *see* it. In short, we need some good examples.

In the fifth century BC, as the mighty Persian army of the east was marching to destroy the various city-states of Greece, the Oracle of Delphi gave a prophecy. She stated a gloomy prediction: "Everything within the borders of Attica shall fall, / Yes, and the sacred vales of nearby mountain ranges, / But the wooden wall alone, the wooden wall shall stand." Later in the prophecy, she stated, "Divine Salamis, you will be the ruin of many a mother's son."[1] The Athenian emissaries could make little sense of what she said. No further explanation was offered. In particular, the phrase about the "wooden wall" was most curious. Could it refer to the wattle fence that in former wars had stood around the rim of the acropolis? The Greek commander Themistocles believed instead that the prophecy referred to ships. Sure enough, although the Persians succeeded in ravaging most of the peninsula, including the Acropolis of Athens itself, the wooden ships of Greece were victorious in repulsing the Persians near the island of Salamis. This proved the turning point, and Greece was saved.

Nearly two millennia later, the term "wooden walls" was being used again, and in much the same context. The tiny island kingdom of England was growing into a mighty world power upon the strength of its navy of wooden battle ships. Time and again throughout its history, England was protected by its "wooden walls" alone. The period during which this occurred, from the Spanish Armada in 1588 to the end of the Napoleonic Wars in 1815, has been called by some scholars "the age of fighting sail." In the broad sweep of world history, it would be difficult to find an era in which the art side of leadership is presented in more colorful relief.

This was one of the fantastic arrays of developments engulfing the globe during this period. World exploration led to global operations. Conquest by land was no longer the only means of national expansion. Conquest through commerce had come of age. As one of the stars of the period, Sir Walter Raleigh wrote while confined in the Tower of London, "Whosoever commands the sea, commands the trade; whosoever commands the trade of the world commands the riches of the world, and consequently the world itself."[2] Wooden ships plied the oceans from east to west and north to south expanding commerce and planting colonies in quest of this world command. Trade flourished and, with it, the mixing of peoples and passions.

Empire building, almost always present in human history, was also underway. The mighty Spanish, Dutch, and Portuguese empires eventually gave way to the emergent French and English. In a dizzying array of wars and changing alliances, the struggle for supremacy grew more and more global in scope.

Religious clashes also took on enormous magnitude, as Catholics and Protestants fought each other for souls and nations. Colonies grew in size and power, overreaching their mother countries and establishing themselves as world contenders in their own right. The age of revolution also dawned during this time, pitching people against their governments and each other. New nations would form, while another would execute its monarchs and crown an emperor.

At the tip of the spear of all this upheaval and change were complicated weapons known as "ships of the line." These gigantic wooden battle ships were some of the most sophisticated and complicated fighting machines the world had yet seen. As Pulitzer Prize–winner Barbara Tuchman wrote:

> Since medieval days of the sixty-pound suit of armor, in which, for the sake of combat, men roasted and could not arise if they fell, no contrivance for fighting has matched in discomfort and inconvenience and use contrary to nature the floating castle called a ship of the line in the age of fighting sail. The difficulties men willingly contend with to satisfy their urge to fight have never been better exemplified than in warships under sail.[3]

According to author Adam Nicolson, "The man-of-war, as complex as a clock, as large as a prison, as delicate as a kite, as strong as a fortress and as murderous as an army, was undoubtedly the most evolved single mechanism, with the most elaborate ordering of parts, the world had ever seen."[4]

By the end of the Napoleonic Wars, ships of the line had swelled to enormous proportions. The HMS *Victory*, which can still be seen in Portsmouth Harbour, England, was representative of flagships at the peak of the age, though it was not the largest. It is 226 feet long and 51 feet abeam, and the tip of its main mast is 205 feet above the waterline. It was constructed from approximately 6,000 trees, most of which were oak, an equivalent to about 100 acres of woodland. Twenty-six miles of cordage was used for the rigging, which could max out at thirty-seven sails covering 6,500 square yards, if needed. In addition to size, ships of the line were also built for strength. Massive wooden ribs and huge bolts provided the structure. Heavy beams bridged the frame internally. Oak planking was used not only for structure and soundness but also as armor, sometimes massing as much as three feet thick.

Figure 1: The Battle of Trafalgar by Javier Turner, highlighting HMS *Victory*

On the larger ships, three stories of guns were mounted along each side, with some guns over nine feet in length and weighing nearly three tons each. Guns were arranged by weight, with the largest mounted on lower decks for sailing stability. The *Victory*, for instance, had 100 guns, with additional small guns on the bow and stern. Varying types of shot could be used, from heavy iron balls for smashing through beams and planks to chain shot for destroying sails and rigging to canister shot, which scattered shrapnel to kill enemy sailors. A ship of the line firing all of its guns down one side at a time, or in rolling succession as the best often did, would be a dangerous adversary. The sound could be literally deafening, the smoke blinding, and the shear velocity and weight of projectiles ferocious and deadly. Although the longer muzzled guns could have a range of well over a mile, most of them were deadliest up close. The bloodiest combination was firing at close range down the length of an enemy vessel, a process called "raking," which many times would clear entire decks the length of a ship of all personnel.

Beyond size, strength, and ferocity, ships of the line were also vehicles capable of sailing to the far reaches of the globe. They could withstand arctic gales, huge waves and swells, winter cold, and tropical heat. Sailing for long periods of time—sometimes years—between dry-dockings for overhauls, the ships had to be self-sufficient and self-sustaining, carrying spare sails and line, timber, and hardware for the never-ending task of maintenance. Repairs afloat were nearly a daily occupation. Considerable skills in navigation were also required, a discipline that saw significant innovation and improvement throughout the age. Demanded also was knowledge of the weather and currents and winds. Charts of shorelines and depths were often suspect at best, and many times, a commander's experience and judgment were all that kept a ship from running aground on a reef, rock, or sand bar. Most ships of the line were square-rigged sailers, meaning the bulk of the sails were mounted perpendicular, or square, to the axis of the ship. This presented large amounts of sail to the wind as was necessary to propel such massive structures, with capable sailing speeds of up to twelve knots. However, square rigging also required large, highly-skilled crews working a complicated system of rigging and blocks to maximize maneuverability.

Specialty skills abounded on board ship, with crewmen assigned to rigging, sails, pumps, navigation, gun crews, the galley, livestock, ship's boats, powder storage and delivery, carpentry, surgery, weapons, and a seemingly endless list of tasks necessary for the smooth operation of a virtual city afloat. At full complement (which was difficult to achieve at war time), a ship like the *Victory* would have a crew of more than 800 men. Some of the largest carried well over a thousand. This necessitated gargantuan supplies of fresh water, food rations, livestock, and alcohol.

Such a large group of people cohabitating in confined space was sure to present its challenges. This is the reason for the strict rules of discipline and harsh punishments of the period. The command structure and the rule of authority had to be absolute. Many of the crew aboard a man-of-war had likely been "pressed" into service, a practice where, on the authority of the crown, a free man would be kidnapped ashore and dragged aboard ship for mandatory service. Most crewmen were illiterate and uneducated. On a typical ship, they would be from many nations and speak different languages. There would be Protestants and Catholics and often Hindus or Muslims from the east aboard. Some were mere children by today's standards: eleven- and twelve-year-olds beginning their life in command as midshipmen.

Class distinctions, of course, were also present. Commanders, in the French and Spanish navies in particular, were almost entirely nobles of "proper birth." Women aboard were mostly considered bad luck, but many are the stories of whores hidden away in the hold. Superstition was rampant, with most crewmen believing in a myriad combination of signs and omens. It was a cacophony of mixed peoples, abilities, and cultures, a strange marriage of man and machine. As former secretary of the navy John Lehman wrote, "Sailors live for months and years inside their weapons."[5]

Atop this staggeringly complex mess strode the captain, supreme and sovereign. At sea for weeks or months or even years at a time, the captain was the sole and complete authority over this amalgam of men. While responsible for smooth operation and order aboard his complicated fighting machine, he was expected to find, harass, contain, or destroy the enemy. This might involve long and arduous blockade duty off an enemy coast or a massive fleet action out at sea. It might require single-ship actions, or it could involve diplomacy in a foreign port. In engaging the enemy, often the hardest part was finding him. Without the technologies of surveillance we take for granted in our military today, captains in the age of fighting sail were forced to rely on a web of spies and informers ashore and lookouts perched atop their masts with spy glasses scanning the distant horizon at sea in addition to their navigation skills. Battles were costly, with the threat of fire or an explosion in the powder room a constant concern. Casualty rates in battle were shockingly high, much more so than for land forces. After an engagement with the enemy, it was often necessary to make repairs for days while bobbing around helplessly at sea. One of the most dangerous combinations was a major battle followed by a storm.

The actual enemy was not the only adversary for a captain of a ship of the line. He was also under orders from his superiors. Often, these orders were ambiguous and political. In every country, the navies of the period were rife with political intrigue and the machinations of ambition. Further, the weather could be as dangerous as any enemy. Storms could scatter and disable entire fleets, putting operational plans and strategic operations entirely aside. Disease, starvation, malnutrition, and thirst could also bring a ship to ruin. Communications were slow and patchy. Many times during the period, national alliances would shift, and it would be weeks or months before captains at sea knew about it. This was further complicated by the fact that many ships disguised their nationality by flying "false colors": the flag of another nation. All this meant that an isolated sea captain, alone in command for extended periods of time, could never be entirely sure who he was to fight.

The amassing of ships into fleets added to the complication. While each ship had its captain, overall command would go to an admiral or commodore. Some fleets were enormous, stretching over miles and miles of sea when underway. In the large fleet battles of the era, the coordination and communication between ships while engaging the enemy were rife with problems. Misunderstandings and confusion were bound to result. In the actual thick of battle, smoke and noise could be so immense that almost no communication was possible. What began as a silent, slow, almost graceful coming together of mighty ships under sail would end in a bedlam of noise, tangled masts, blood, gore, and death.

It is against this remarkable backdrop that we may see true leadership displayed in ways most interesting and instructive. Facing such challenges operationally, tactically, and strategically, the need for leadership in this historic era was monumental. It is when challenges are the greatest, when pressures are the highest, when risk is at its maximum, that the real mettle of leaders is revealed. Men who could rise above such demanding circumstances as those in the age of fighting sail and lead others to accomplishment are truly worthy of study. In their time, so foreign from ours, and in how and why they did what they did, there is much to learn.

Unfortunately, women play a small role in this study, as would be expected from an era that largely excluded them from positions of public prominence. However, their influence on some of the major characters will be clearly seen and felt.

It should be noted that this is not an authoritative history book. It will not flow chronologically through the era. It will also avoid the temptation to historical completeness of including each of the major naval engagements of the period. Nor will it follow the common tactic of relating an historical event and then culling random principles from that story. Instead, its aim is to bring to light the art side of leadership against the colorful backdrop of the characters and struggles of the time. Events that illustrate similar traits within a category of leadership will be presented together. In this way of studying multiple sides of the same principle, as illustrated by the gallant and not-so-gallant leaders of the age of fighting sail, not only the high points of the lesson but also its ever-important subtleties should come to light. It is hoped, however, that in addition to heightened leadership ability, the reader gains an understanding of and an interest in a fascinating part of our shared history.

Now, let us beat to quarters and clear the decks for action!

CHAPTER ONE

The Lesson of the Ripple Effect

Leadership Principle:

Leadership matters. It makes a difference. In fact, its results cannot really be measured. A leader's influence spreads through society and time and often has a much bigger effect than might be imagined. This is called the ripple effect. Remember, a forest fire starts with just a tiny spark. The tallest oak grows from a small acorn. So it is with the efforts and influence of a leader. Decisions have consequences. Actions have corresponding results. One person can and does make a difference—and sometimes a *huge* difference.

Illustration #1: Sir Sidney Smith and the Siege of Acre

The year was 1798. Napoleon Bonaparte was on the rise and had been granted command of a great army to conquer Egypt and, from there, penetrate eastward and form a grand French empire. Napoleon and his army had made landfall, but shortly afterward, his fleet of ships was destroyed by Nelson at the Battle of the Nile. Napoleon was effectively stranded, forced to press ahead with his plans with limitations on supply and reinforcement.

That same year, Englishman Sir Sidney Smith was being held in the high-security Temple prison in Paris, having been captured in a naval engagement and suspected of being a spy. Smith was indeed a spy, a propagandist, and an expert at psychological warfare as well. Into the ceiling of his jail cell he inscribed:

> Fortune's wheel makes strange revolutions, it must be confessed; but for the term revolution to be applicable, the turn of the wheel should be complete. You are today as high as you can be. Very well. I envy not your good fortune, for mine is better still. I am as low in the career of ambition as a man can well descend; so that, let this capricious dame, fortune, turn her wheel ever so little—I must necessarily mount, for the same reason that you must descend.[1]

His remarks, which found widespread coverage in newspapers, were aimed at Napoleon. At that moment, it must have seemed inconceivable that one man in such a low position would ever be able to make good on what had become known as "Smith's Prophecy." But incredibly, Sir Sidney Smith managed to escape the Temple prison. Following the Battle of the Nile, he was ordered to sail his eighty-gun ship *Tigre* to Constantinople on a diplomatic mission to bring the Turks and Russians into an alliance with England to defend against Napoleon's advancing army. Smith also managed to obtain secret intelligence of Napoleon's troop movements and objectives and patched together a force of French Royalists (native Frenchmen opposed to the government then in charge of their country).

As Napoleon's army marched into Syria slaughtering enemies and civilians alike, Smith sailed into Acre with two ships and built an alliance with the town's ruler, Ahmed Jezzar Pasha. By the time Napoleon's army arrived at the outskirts of Acre, with no way around that would not leave his rear in danger, Smith and his sailors, Turkish soldiers, and French Royalists had fortified the harbor and walls of the city. Two English warships were in the harbor along with several gun boats. As Napoleon's ships arrived with his siege artillery, they were captured by the English. Napoleon continued to feel the sting of the loss of his fleet at the Battle of the Nile. Now he would be forced to take Acre without his heaviest artillery. Smith was exploiting every opportunity.

Although fewer than 5,000 defenders made up Smith's blended force, their morale was high as the roughly 10,000 French troops dug in for a siege of the city. Smith had worked his diplomatic magic with the inhabitants of the surrounding countryside, making it difficult for Napoleon's troops to get supplies, information, or any kind of support. In the battle to win the hearts of the local population, despite Napoleon's claims of liberation and freedom, Smith had already won.

The French first attacked what appeared to be a small breach in the protective walls around Acre, but Smith had already plugged the breach and added extra guns to it for protection. The French were repulsed. While Smith was gone on affairs in Naples, the French attacked again but failed. Next, they attempted to tunnel under the city walls and plant explosives, but this had so far only cost French lives. Napoleon grew increasingly frustrated, the rich Silk Road out of his reach until he could reduce Acre, and all the while, his supplies and men were dwindling. Napoleon's resolve, however, had not yet flagged. He told Bourrienne:

> I see that this wretched dump has cost me a good number of men, and wasted much time. But things are too far advanced not to attempt one last effort. If I succeed...I shall find in the town the pasha's treasures, and weapons for 300,000 men. I will stir up and arm all of Syria...I will march on Damascus and Aleppo...I will reach Constantinople with a huge army. I will overthrow the Turkish Empire. I will found in the East a new and great Empire that will ensure my place in posterity.[2]

Such bombast might sound ridiculous if it came from almost anyone else. But knowing what we know of the next seventeen years of Napoleon's life, his words give a steel clarity to the difficulty Smith was facing.

In response, Smith's industry in repulsing the French was hands-on and energetic. In the words of authors Roy and Lesley Adkins, "Smith seemed to be everywhere at once, constantly moving from his flagship, where he directed the naval operations and tried to maintain correspondence, into the city to lead the fighting on the walls during the assaults, and even outside the city on reconnaissance missions."[3] The eleventh and final attack of the siege was not lead by Napoleon. He had been counseled to stay behind. But standing on the front line of the defense, right in the gap in the wall, was Sir Sidney Smith. Again, the attack was turned back.

Smith, as if to close a chapter, actually wrote a letter to Napoleon after the withdrawal of the French, in which he said:

> ...circumstances remind me to wish that you would reflect on the instability of human affairs. In fact, could you have thought that a poor prisoner in a cell of the Temple prison—that an unfortunate for whom you refused, for a single moment, to give yourself any concern, being at the same time able to render him a signal service, since you were then all-powerful—could you have thought, I say, that this same man would have become your antagonist, and have compelled you, in the midst of the sands of Syria, to raise the siege of a miserable, almost defenseless town? Such events, you must admit, exceed all human calculations. Believe me, general...

that Asia is not a theatre made for your glory. This letter is a little revenge that I give myself.[4]

Napoleon retreated to Egypt with nearly a third of his force depleted. According to Roy and Lesley Adkins, "Napoleon might not have made it as far as India, but it is quite likely he would have been left in control of Syria and the Silk Road trade route....Acre was the first defeat on land for the so-called invincible general."[5] Eventually, events back in France would cause Napoleon to steal away to Europe and leave the remainder of his force almost literally stranded in Africa, his dreams of an Empire of the East killed by many factors, chief among them a determined and unlikely adversary.

Understanding and Application

Sir Sidney Smith, although an accomplished and decorated man, found himself stripped of his power and freedom. Nonetheless, he dared to envision a day when the "wheel of fortune" would return him to a position of influence. His daring led to action, and his action led to results. Napoleon's vision of an eastern empire was dead forever. Smith's pluck, energy, and determination proved a formidable combination against one of history's brightest commanders.

As leaders fulfill their responsibilities, fighting against seemingly insurmountable odds, meeting challenges and obstacles, it is critical to remember that one person can and does make a difference. It might take everything a leader has to offer. It might require time and sacrifice. It may be extremely difficult. The results may or may not even show up during one's lifetime, but a leader operates under the foundational belief that his or her efforts matter. Leaders do what they can, with what they've got, where they are, as Theodore Roosevelt instructed.[6] Futility is a foreign concept to leaders. Perhaps Sir Sidney Smith said it best: "It is the greatest of all mistakes to do nothing because you can only do a little. Do what you can."[7] Do what you can, indeed, and let the ripple effect handle the rest.

Illustration #2: Captain Samuel C. Reid at the Battle of Fayal

In the long and rich history of the age of fighting sail, *privateers* were civilian sailing vessels that had been given governmental approval to make war at will upon enemy shipping. Privateers could thus both claim patriotism and wealth while inflicting pain on an enemy nation. Privateering was very popular and very effective; in a way, it was the nautical version of today's guerilla terrorism, with a bit of a mercenary touch.

In the War of 1812 between Great Britain and the infantile United States, a war many called the second war of independence, American privateers wreaked havoc upon the mighty British. Perhaps surprisingly, their efforts against the crown were far more successful than those of the relatively small American navy. According to author John Lehman, "During the War there were 513 registered privateers and they took about 2,300 British merchant ships compared to 165 taken by the Navy."[8] That means that the average American privateer captured or destroyed more than four enemy ships each!

One of these privateering vessels was captained by Samuel C. Reid. Reid's story makes the case that one man's efforts can have a staggering impact, with ramifications that are unforeseen at the time.

Reid was captain of the *General Armstrong*, a schooner mounting only nine guns and having a crew of about ninety men. Reid and his crew were able to break out of the British blockade of New York in a dead calm by pumping water on the sails to capture all possible wind and by towing the ship with rowboats. He sailed to Fayal harbor in the Azores and arrived just before a British squadron of three battle ships of varying size and armament. The squadron was on its way to New Orleans with British troops to assist in the attack on the city. First, however, seeing the *General Armstrong* in Fayal, the squadron decided to violate Portuguese neutrality and attack the American privateer.

The first wave of attack consisted of several small boats from the British squadron. When they failed to take the *General Armstrong*, the next attack went in at midnight with fourteen boats and 600 men. Many of these attackers were successful in climbing aboard the *General Armstrong*. The battle entailed fierce hand-to-hand combat. Casualties were high, and Reid himself killed the commander of the raid. Once again, the British attack was repulsed. Expecting another attempt, Reid moved his ship closer to the shore so he could use the guns from both sides of his ship on one side. He cut new gun ports in the hull and aimed his full complement of weapons seaward.

In the early morning, the smallest of the three ships in the British squadron attacked, primarily because it could come in closest to shore without running aground. In a raging battle of the cannon from both ships, the British ship was forced to back off. At this point, the British had had enough. They next maneuvered their largest battleship in the squadron, a full seventy-eight-gun man-of-war, into position to bombard the tiny American privateer. Reid countered by setting fire to his own ship and sinking it rather than letting the enemy capture it. His men escaped to safety ashore. In the entirety of the engagement, some four distinct skirmishes, the British suffered thirty-four killed and sixty-eight wounded. Of the Americans, only two were killed and seven wounded. The little ship had held out remarkably well against superior firepower and numbers. In a gesture illustrative of the chivalry between officers occasionally found in wars in those times, the British Consulate on shore invited Captain Reid to tea, where he was given three cheers by the surviving British officers for his bravery and gallantry in the battle.

Understanding and Application

Reid was doing his duty. He took responsibility for commanding his tiny schooner to the best of his ability and putting up a stiff resistance to a fierce enemy under hopeless odds. His crew fought viciously and creatively in a complicated warship under dangerous conditions — proof of good leadership and unity. As a leader, Captain Reid did was what required, when it was required, to the best of his ability.

What Captain Reid could not have foreseen, however, as is true with many in leadership, is the enormous ramifications of his gallant stand at the Battle of Fayal. His efforts delayed the British expedition against New Orleans for ten days. The extra time allowed General Andrew Jackson to arrive on scene in New Orleans; take martial control of the panicked town; assemble his patch-work army of pirates, militia, and escaped slaves; and prepare his defenses. What resulted was the most lop-sided battle of the entire war, as the British were badly defeated. The Battle of New Orleans could have ended differently. Andrew Jackson later told Captain Reid himself, "If there had been no Battle of Fayal, there would have been no Battle of New Orleans."[9] Had that happened, the tentative treaty that had already been signed to end the war most likely would have been revoked or at least amended less favorably to the United States, keeping the door open to future hostility. Instead, it sealed the deal on a lasting peace between the two nations.

The leadership of Captain Reid and his stand at the Battle of Fayal clearly illustrates the difference that one person can make. How easy would it have been for Reid to simply flee from the enemy in his tiny, much faster ship? How easily could he have fired a few shots in defense, as was customary in hopeless situations, and then "hauled down his colors" and surrendered? Or he could have simply abandoned his ship and escaped to shore. But Reid chose to stand and fight, and his men with him. That simple decision, and its gallant execution, made a huge difference on the world's stage.

That is the kind of far-reaching effect that one person can have. That is the difference leadership makes. If Reid hadn't stood, if his men hadn't fought, if they hadn't delayed the British, then General Jackson might not have been ready, the British may have prevailed in the Battle of New Orleans, and Western history might be different. But they stood. Reid led. And it made all the difference.

In a complicated world, with forces for change coming at us from seemingly all directions, it is easy to feel small and incapable. It is easy to shrug off our highest aspirations and think, "What's the use?" This becomes doubly tempting when meeting challenges and when our best intentions turn out to be more difficult and more work than we expected. At that point, it is more critical than ever to realize that we as individuals have enormous power to not only influence the course of events around us but also to have a major and lasting effect on the impact of those events.

Illustration #3: The Battle of the Bay and the Birth of a Nation

The War for American Independence had dragged on for six long years. General George Washington and his beleaguered troops had hung on just about as long as humanly possible. Without the much-needed infusion of troops, supplies, and money from the French government, the colonial resistance would have faltered long before. Barbara Tuchman wrote:

> The French, who had put large expectations in the abasement of Britain that American success would cause, had been disappointed by the weakness of the American military effort. Instead of an aggressive ally, they were tied to a dependent client, unable to establish a strong government and requiring transfusions of men-at-arms and money to keep its war effort alive. The Americans were notified that the French government had already spent more than "Congress had a right to expect from the friendship of their ally."[10]

For the colonial war effort, time was running out.

The British, too, were tiring of the struggle. The cost of the war and its growing unpopularity back in London were mounting. It was as if each side were holding on, hoping for a lucky knock-out blow. That blow would come in the late summer of 1781 in a coordination of land and sea forces that historian Don Higginbotham called "virtually unparalleled in the history of eighteenth-century warfare."[11]

British Lieutenant General Lord Charles Cornwallis had won a costly victory at Guilford Courthouse in North Carolina. However, as he operated throughout the south, far away from supply lines and harassed by colonials, he was forced to retreat to the shores of Virginia to await either reinforcements or removal by ship and subsequent transport back to the British base in New York. Colonial General George Washington and his French ally Lieutenant General Jean-Baptiste-Donatien de Vimeur, comte de Rochambeau, saw Cornwallis's precarious position as the chance for which they had been waiting. Although two previous attempts to combine naval and land forces had failed, the two commanders concocted an elaborate plan, with multiple moving parts, to coordinate both land and sea efforts and bring a concentration of force to bear on Cornwallis and encircle and entrap him in Yorktown, Virginia. If it worked, it could be the major battle victory that was so desperately needed for the colonial cause.

Both the French and British navies were divided into squadrons and dispersed around the globe for protection of commerce and the guarding of ports and colonies, as well as to keep an eye on each other. At the strategic and operational levels, it was extremely important to balance power against the enemy and concentrate enough force where necessary to ensure victory and escape destruction of portions of the fleet. In the age of fighting sail, so much was dependent on numbers of ships engaged and the concentration of force. Leading up to the Battle of Yorktown, a massive game of fleet movements preceded the actual battle and played a crucial role in its outcome.

A large French fleet commanded by Vice-Admiral François-Joseph-Paul, comte de Grasse was in the Caribbean (the West Indies). De Grasse had sailed from France earlier in the year with orders to intervene in some way in the American Revolution using the West Indies as his base. Upon arriving in the Caribbean, de Grasse had expertly outmaneuvered an English fleet and had secured French bases there. He gathered troops and financial support and even decided to foot the bill for transport ships out of his own pocket. De Grasse next negotiated with the Spanish, getting them to agree to protect the Antilles islands without French help for a short time, leaving him free to take his entire fleet north to America. He then bargained for troops that had been on loan from the French government, borrowing them for the coming action. De Grasse had made the decision to take his entire fleet, armed with troops and supply ships, to fight in the American effort.

This was incredible for many reasons. First, it meant that he was abandoning his duty to protect the lucrative West Indies, which most in Europe at that time viewed as being much more important than anything in North America. Second, it required him to forego the protection of convoys of French commerce heading back to Europe, a move guaranteed to win him criticism and censure from the powerful merchants back home. Tuchman wrote, "We do not know what de Grasse thought or felt, and can only judge by his subsequent dedication of himself and his fortune to a faltering cause not his own."[12] De Grasse wrote a letter to Rochambeau and Washington alerting them that he was sailing with a full fleet and troops and would meet them at the Chesapeake in Virginia.

A smaller French fleet, which had transported the French army of Rochambeau to North America, was stationed in Rhode Island and commanded by Louis the comte de Barras. It contained the artillery and ammunition that would be needed for a siege of Cornwallis. De Barras was to sail south from Rhode Island and rendezvous with de Grasse, if he could escape the British navy's blockade of the North American coast.

On the English side, Rear-Admiral Thomas Graves had recently been given command of the fleet at New York. Graves had never commanded a ship in a major battle, much less an entire fleet. In the Caribbean, the large English fleet was under the command of Admiral Sir George Brydges Rodney, a fighting admiral who was at the time suffering so badly from a prostate infection that he was increasingly unable to command.

The British had been made aware of the intentions of the French to deliver naval support to the Americans, but their intelligence didn't tell them where or how. As a result, they were on alert both in the North American station and in the West Indies. While cruising on June 5, Rodney actually sighted de Grasse's fleet at sea but made the fateful decision not to engage or pursue. Rodney felt it more important to protect English holdings in the Caribbean and the incoming convoys from Britain and Ireland than to risk battle with de Grasse at that point. He was also quite sure de Grasse would divide his fleet and send only a portion of it north to the Americans. For that reason, Rodney dispatched Admiral Sir Samuel Hood with fourteen ships of the line (battleships) and five frigates (smaller, faster ships used for scouting and communication) to pursue de Grasse. Rodney correctly guessed de Grasse's final destination, so he instructed Hood to combine forces with Graves in New York and meet de Grasse before he could bottle up Cornwallis in Yorktown.

Rodney, perhaps the one British commander who understood the magnitude of what was about to happen, grew increasingly ill and abandoned any attempt at leading a squadron of his own and instead sailed home to England for medical attention. This would prove significant, as it deprived the English of not only two much needed ships (and one frigate) but of the one man who had figured out exactly what the French were up to and where they would bring it to fruition.

Rodney sent a warning letter to Graves in New York letting him know of the French intentions and making him aware that Hood was sailing north to join him. In a twist of history as significant as Rodney's debilitating health and his refusal to engage de Grasse earlier that summer, the message was intercepted by American privateers and was never delivered. Hood also sent a warning letter ahead to Graves, but this too was captured at sea. Also, Rodney sent an order to another English commander in the Caribbean to dispatch five more ships (and five more frigates) to sail north and assist in the effort, but the order was inexplicably disobeyed. The ships never sailed to help.

In order to avoid detection on his way to America, de Grasse had taken a difficult and dangerously slow route through the Bahama Channel. It was a move no one expected. When Hood reached the Chesapeake with his ships, he had passed de Grasse's fleet without knowing it and arrived there ahead of him. As Hood looked in at the Chesapeake and saw it devoid of any enemy ships, he immediately sailed onward to New York to meet up with Graves. Hood informed Graves of Rodney's suspicions about the French fleet's intent to encircle Cornwallis in Yorktown off the Chesapeake. On the same day, a message came in that de Barras's French fleet had escaped the blockade of Newport, Rhode Island, and had disappeared out to sea.

At this point, there seemed to be some confusion in the British command about whether or not the French meant to instead attack New York. There were now two French fleets at large, and nobody knew for sure where they were headed. Finally, after much wrangling, the English commanders decided to sail with their combined strength back to the Chesapeake and relieve Cornwallis's army, acting on what Rodney had intended all along. For some unexplained reason, however, they waited for three days before beginning the complicated process of maneuvering their fleet around the treacherous waters of Sandy Hook, which in itself was a three-day project.

While all of this was happening at sea, Washington and Rochambeau were fast-marching their armies from the north down to Virginia, and a small contingent of colonial forces under General Lafayette were doing their best to keep Cornwallis pinned in place. Again, inexplicably, the

British forces in New York under General Sir Henry Clinton paid little attention to the movements of the American and French armies as they passed, even when they were each in turn dangerously exposed during a ferry crossing of the nearby North River.

Before Hood and Graves had even decided to sail out of New York to Cornwallis's rescue, de Grasse had arrived in the Chesapeake with twenty-eight ships of the line and 3,000 troops. When Admiral Graves finally arrived on the scene, he was dumbstruck to find the French fleet there in all its strength and not the smaller divided fleet he had expected. The masts from the French ships were so numerous they looked like a forest. However, even though de Grasse's fleet had superior numbers, Graves was in a very advantageous position. The wind was in his favor, his squadron was sailing in good order, and he had caught de Grasse in ragged formation, maneuvering his ships out of the bay after having offloaded his troops and supplies. Graves had the perfect opportunity to overwhelm the French fleet and wreak massive destruction.

Experts agree that if Graves would have bored down upon the French and attacked their ships one by one as they rounded the corner to the bay, he would have won a decisive victory. But Graves attempted instead to fight the battle in what was called the "line ahead" formation. This tactic had been codified into the *Fighting Instructions* used to train all fleet movements for the British navy and had been developed and handed down for generations. It was official procedure and the accepted and even expected practice of battle engagement. Line ahead basically involved arranging all the battle ships of the fleet in single file and sailing up alongside the similarly arranged line of enemy ships, firing away as they passed. Originally, it had proven a very effective fighting technique under the right conditions, bringing order out of chaos.

But Graves's situation that day didn't present itself quite as neatly as the procedure required. Because the French fleet of de Grasse was in ragged formation and just coming out of the bay, it was not in a line at all and would therefore not cooperate with a line-to-line battle. Further, the signal system used by the British navy at the time, with its complicated, difficult-to-see flags and its ambiguity, was a major cause of confusion.

None of Graves's ship captains could figure out just how he intended for them to engage the enemy. To make matters worse, Graves himself didn't seem to know what to do. He wasted almost two-and-a-half hours before he made the signal to engage the enemy. He at first signaled for the line ahead formation, and then he sent up the signal for everyone to engage the nearest enemy but left up the first signal as well. With the two signals flying at the same time, some captains obeyed the second, while others stayed with the first. The result was that only a portion of Graves's vanguard (the ships at the front of the line of his fleet) came into contact with the enemy. Frustrated, Graves tried to lead by example by maneuvering his own ship in a way that everyone could mimic. This caused even more confusion, as some ships followed his lead, and others didn't. Also, Admiral Hood, who was commanding the ships in the rear of Graves's fleet, didn't see the signal to engage, so his ships were never brought to bear on the enemy at all. Hood instead followed the ships ahead of him intending to come into battle in line ahead formation, which never happened.

After bringing only ten of the nineteen British ships of the line into battle with eleven of the twenty-four French battle ships and noticing the late hour of the day, Graves decided to break off the battle. For the next two days, the fleets remained in sight of each other but didn't engage, using the time to make repairs to their damaged ships instead. The next day, Graves and his English fleet departed the scene and sailed back to New York. De Grasse, the strategic victor of the Battle of the Bay if not the tactical one, promptly sailed back into the harbor and prepared for the siege of Cornwallis.

It was now Cornwallis's turn to make inexplicable moves. After learning of the outcome of the Battle of the Bay (sometimes called the Battle of the Capes), Cornwallis had plenty of time to retreat. With a decisive strike against Lafayette's little force, Cornwallis could have escaped his trap and moved his troops to safer ground. But he chose to stay put.

The end was now at hand. De Barras, commander of the other French fleet, showed up right on time a couple days after the Battle of the Bay with siege guns and food supplies. Washington and Rochambeau, after a herculean march, were on scene, making the envelopment of Cornwallis complete. With no reinforcements from sea and no means of escape, Cornwallis was trapped. A complicated operation, requiring the coordination of multiple land and sea units of newly-allied forces speaking different languages with different fighting cultures and little or no communication, had done the nearly impossible.

With the surrender of Cornwallis, the War for American Independence was effectively over. Even though negotiations didn't conclude in a peace treaty for two more years, the Americans had won their independence and been granted the chance to form a new nation, and Great Britain had forever lost its most valuable colonies.

Understanding and Application

Even attempting to tell the story of the envelopment and victory at Yorktown is a complicated affair. There are so many individuals, armies, and fleets to be considered, and that's partly the point. It was a multidimensional effort, short on odds of success and relying upon the leadership performance of many parties. The French and Americans in alliance rose brilliantly to the challenge of leadership. The British failed miserably.

Admiral Graves's complicity in the loss must first be considered. From his point of view, he had many things to consider as he sailed into battle that day off the mouth of the Chesapeake. Author Michael A. Palmer wrote, "Graves' responsibilities included both the extraction of Cornwallis and, more important, the survival of his fleet, upon which depended the security of the army in New

York and Canada and the island colonies in the West Indies." Further, perhaps due to his lack of command experience in battle, Graves demonstrated a restricting adherence to procedure that stifled the fighting effectiveness of his squadron. He also had not had time to communicate with his ship captains prior to the engagement, and they quite simply didn't understand what he wanted them to do, nor did they perform well individually. As Palmer wrote, "Whatever the imperfections of Graves' scheme of battle, his well-intentioned efforts were undermined by the poor judgment and execution of his subordinates."[13]

Conversely, de Grasse's decision to strike at the Chesapeake was brilliant strategically. It brought a concentration of forces on an enemy that had maneuvered itself into a tight spot. But much more critical was de Grasse's incredible and risky decision not to divide his fleet but rather to sail it in full strength away from his station in the Caribbean and to the aid of the American cause. This bold stroke proved to be one of the deciding factors in the birth of a nation.

Rodney's decision not to engage de Grasse when he had spotted him in the Caribbean proved fatal. How much of Rodney's usual fighting spirit had been reduced by his failing health can never be ascertained. But it can be said with some certainty that if Rodney had engaged de Grasse while he had him in the Caribbean, the siege of Yorktown likely never would have happened. Sea battles were usually quite damaging to both sides, and de Grasse would have been hard pressed to launch an offensive so far away following even a victorious encounter with Rodney. Further, if Rodney's health had held out long enough to allow him to get into the battle at the Chesapeake, as he attempted to do, things might still have turned out differently. As Admiral Hood said of the battle, "Had that admiral [Rodney] led his Majesty's squadron from the West Indies to this coast, the 5th of September would I think have been a most glorious day for Great Britain."[14] Considering that just one year later Rodney won a sensational victory over de Grasse at the Battle of the Saintes, Hood was likely correct.

Of George Washington's heroic decision, perhaps Tuchman said it best:

> The opportunity to combine his land forces with French naval power to enclose Cornwallis in the vulnerable position he had chosen at Yorktown would be, Washington realized, his one chance to defeat the enemy and bring a culmination to the long struggle. To conduct his own forces into place to do the job would be a task of extraordinary difficulty and would involve a serious risk of failure — of his own reputation, of his army and of the cause of independence. It required a decision as bold as Hannibal's to cross the Alps by elephant. Washington took it without visible hesitation.[15]

British General Clinton in New York made a major blunder when he allowed the armies of Washington and

Rochambeau to pass by unmolested. He further aggravated the situation when he dallied before sending Graves and Hood south to Cornwallis's aid.

Cornwallis put the final nail in the coffin when he refused to attempt a retreat after the loss of the sea battle even though it should have been obvious that help could not reach him. As Tuchman wrote, "In truth, a month of paralysis took hold of the British command in America when the French fleet entered the situation, as if the three — Clinton, the Commander-in-Chief; Graves, the Naval Chief; Cornwallis, General of the Army on the spot — had been administered a sedative."[16]

Finally, the independent action of privateers that intercepted the messages from Rodney and Hood cannot be forgotten. History seems to turn on such small acts of initiative.

From all of this, it can clearly be seen that the decisions and actions of a leader make a difference, and many times, the impact is enormous. Leadership matters. The bold and gutsy decisions of the French and American allies proved monumentally successful. De Grasse's gamble not to divide his fleet, Washington's willingness to risk everything, and the pesky performance of the American privateers all played major roles in victory. Conversely, the failure of leadership on the part of the various British commanders was devastating. The results of the choices and performance of the leaders involved in the Yorktown campaign are staggering. Based on what they did, a war was concluded, a nation was born, and the world's geopolitical balance was forever changed.

Also, through the broad sweep of this bit of history, we can see again and again that one person can and does make a difference. Even when embroiled in a complicated, multinational, multicontinental operation, events still turned on the decisions and actions of *individuals*. A leader must never lose sight of the fact that he or she can make a difference. While the smoke of battle rages and confusion abounds, when efforts seem miniscule compared to the big picture, when critics and enemies are all around, a leader must hold true to the belief that his or her efforts *matter*.

Summary

Leaders are dealers in action. They do what they do because they want, and often need, to craft a certain result. Leaders assault the status quo in service of a vision for something more, different, just, bigger, or better. Leaders do this because they know that what they do makes a difference in outcomes. Often, as in the case of the Battle of the Bay, a leader's actions and decisions interact with those of other leaders to become part of a bigger picture of results. This coordination leads to the multiplication of the effects of leadership.

And yet there is something more. The effects of leadership can multiply and grow exponentially, changing and improving circumstances and situations beyond the realm of the first look, cascading across organizations and space and even down through time. This is called the ripple effect. Understanding it should be a great encouragement to leaders, who must realize that they should do what they can do because their contribution will likely outrun their ability to measure it.

CHAPTER TWO

The Lesson of Hunger

Leadership Principle:

Leadership begins and ends with hunger. The hunger of an individual to risk his or her own personal comfort and affluence and attack the status quo is not only the initiation of leadership but also its sustaining force.

Hunger, it should be noted, is different from ambition. Where ambition is largely about self-aggrandizement, hunger is more about service and significance. This type of leader — the true, authentic kind — is unable to leave well enough alone. He or she must assault what he or she observes to be an unacceptable status quo, often at great risk to self. Such leaders are more willing to compromise their comfort than their principles.

This is precisely why leadership is so inspiring. Conversely, when hunger wanes, by definition, a person's leadership wanes along with it. When the status quo becomes increasingly acceptable, a leader's influence diminishes correspondingly.

Illustration #1: Horatio Nelson's Teenage Decision

The history of the age of fighting sail is full of many fascinating and colorful characters, men whose bravery and intelligence impacted the flow of events and the strength of nations. One man, however, dominates the scene.

Horatio Nelson was born the son of an Anglican priest and lost his mother when he was nine. With the help of an uncle, Nelson joined the Royal Navy at age twelve and thus started one of the most illustrious careers of any man in any navy in any age. But just as the pages of history often reveal, it could have been much different.

At age seventeen, while on the West Indies station aboard the frigate *Dolphin*, Nelson fell desperately sick with malaria. Contemporaries noted that he looked like a skeleton, and in a desperate moment, Nelson made a decision. He later wrote of it:

> I felt impressed with the idea that I should never rise in my profession. My mind was staggered with a view of the difficulties I had to surmount, and the little interest I possessed. I could discover no means of reaching the object of my ambitions. After a long and gloomy reverie, in which I almost wished myself overboard, a sudden glow of patriotism was kindled within me, and presented my king and country as my patron. My mind exulted in the idea. "Well, then" I exclaimed, "I will be a hero, and, confiding in Providence, I will brave every danger."[1]

According to author Michael A. Palmer, "There then appeared in Nelson's 'mind's eye...a radiant orb...which urged him on to renown.'"[2]

Nelson seems to say that achievement for its own sake was too large a goal to attain, given his challenges of lowly position and lack of connections. However, when he happened upon the idea that his efforts would be focused on patriotism and serving his king, that thought of "otherness" brought him inspiration. Spurred on by his renewed dedication, he became a captain before age twenty-one and was world-famous by his late thirties. He was principally involved in some of the most enormous naval victories in British history, including the Battle of the Nile in 1798, Copenhagen in 1801, and Trafalgar in 1805, each of which saw the near destruction of an entire enemy fleet. And not only was he instrumental in the development of many other extremely capable and successful commanders, but he also fostered a prevalent culture that many would claim persists in the Royal Navy to this day.

Whether one takes Nelson's words, written later, at face value or not, the fact remains that his near-death experience as a youth inspired him immensely. Many people, when confronted bluntly by their own mortality, determine to make their lives count for something. The focusing of Nelson's hunger upon a cause bigger than himself became, at least according to him, the source of the greatness of his later achievements.

Illustration #2: John Paul Jones

Theodore Roosevelt called legendary John Paul Jones the father of the American navy. Every schoolchild knows that it was Jones who purportedly uttered the famous words, "I have not yet begun to fight."[3] The facts are even more interesting than the legend.

Jones was born John Paul in Scotland in 1747, son of a gardener and domestic servant. He first went to sea at age thirteen as a cabin boy in the British Merchant Marine. Later, when the ship he served on was sold, he transferred to a slave ship. Leaving that position in disgust, John Paul next, through a chain of events, became master of a brig at age twenty-one. A disobedient carpenter named Mungo Maxwell gave John Paul consistent trouble, and, as was customary and lawful at the time, John Paul ordered that Maxwell be flogged with a cat-o'-nine-tails. Maxwell shortly transferred to another ship and, although appearing healthy, died before the ship reached England. As a result, Maxwell's father filed murder charges against John Paul, but the charges were later dropped.

Years later in Tobago, John Paul was faced with a mutinous crew. In the standoff, John Paul fatally stabbed the ringleader with a sword. Fearing an unfair trial in the small community, he fled the island on another ship, leaving his belongings and identity behind and eventually finding his way to Virginia. There appears to be evidence that John Paul then had an illicit affair with a Dorothea Dandridge, who later married Patrick Henry. When the American Revolutionary War broke out, John Paul, who had by then assumed the alias John Jones, was commissioned a first lieutenant in the Continental Navy.

His first command brought him much success, and he was soon promoted to the rank of captain. Jones sailed to France, met with Benjamin Franklin, and was given orders to harass English shipping in their own waters. His ensuing efforts were brave and aggressive. Although strategically insignificant, Jones's coastal raids and attacks on English shipping brought massive psychological pressure in England. He soon gained the reputation among the English of a fearsome pirate, and the anti-war efforts in Parliament were significantly strengthened.

In 1779, Jones, now famous in France, was given a heavily armed merchant ship, which he named the *Bonhomme Richard*. It was aboard this ship that he encountered the British two-decker called the *Serapis*. The far more powerful and numerous guns of the *Serapis* soon reduced the *Bonhomme Richard* to a mere wreck. But somehow Jones managed to maneuver his smaller craft alongside the *Serapis* and use grappling hooks to connect the two ships. With only three guns still working, Jones's situation looked helpless. It was at this point, when the British yelled across to ask for his surrender, that Jones is said to have shouted his famous words.

Indeed, the colonials were not yet finished. Sharpshooters aboard the *Bonhomme Richard* were picking off British sailors continuously. A grenade was dropped from the yardarm high above the *Bonhomme Richard's* deck and into the hold of the *Serapis*, causing an enormous explosion. Finally, the *Serapis* was forced to surrender. The *Bonhomme Richard* soon sunk, and Jones and his crew sailed their prize back to port.

Jones became an instant hero and legend. Upon returning to the colonies, he was given command of a new full-sized ship of the line, which was under construction. Unfortunately for a man of action like Jones, it was not completed until after the war was over, and worse, it was then given to France. Without a command, Jones was dealt the further insult, in his mind, of not being made an admiral. The Continental Congress voted to award Jones a medal, but it was never given to him. His ideas of the organization of a new American navy were also largely ignored.

Frustrated and feeling snubbed, he took a job commanding the Russian navy, where he encountered even more vile politics. Jones died embittered and alone, angry at what he felt was mistreatment at the hands of two governments and never having become a United States citizen.

Understanding and Application

Horatio Nelson and John Paul Jones are both complicated and interesting personalities. They were both brave and ferocious in battle, each grasping a clear picture of the larger strategies and possessing the ability to successfully lead men in the most dangerous of conditions. The motivating force behind their achievements was their hunger for something more.

As I wrote with coauthor Orrin Woodward in our book *Launching a Leadership Revolution*, there are three main levels of hunger. The first level is material success, the motivation of financial gain and monetary prosperity. The second and more powerful level is recognition and respect. The third and deepest level is a cause greater than one's self, an overriding sense of purpose, and the desire to leave a legacy.

Various levels of hunger were at work in the lives of both Nelson and Jones. Both men were born to humble parents of little financial standing, and in a world where class distinction presented barriers more difficult to surmount than any we encounter in our age, military glory was one of the clearest paths upward. Both men were driven for personal glory and the respect and recognition that were perhaps even more desired in their time than in our own. In the case of Jones, he appears to have been a bit more prickly than most, consistently scuffling with others over his honor and perceived slights. While this was doubtlessly a large part of his motivation, it was also one of his biggest weaknesses and the cap on the magnitude of his success. Nelson claimed to have become motivated by something bigger than himself—proclaiming patriotism and a zeal for his king that our modern ears have trouble taking as sincere. Both men were cognizant of their standing in history and seemed to be looking forward to how they would be remembered.

Digging into someone's personal motivations is always a tricky and complicated affair. We can never know for sure what someone was thinking or feeling. Sometimes, leaders are not even clear about their own motivations. But we can find clues by studying the lives of brave and successful leaders like Nelson and Jones. These clues can then be fashioned into a map of our own motivational territory. Leaders would do well to analyze their own motivations, making sure their source of hunger is healthy and productive because, although a motivation for respect and recognition can be productive, it is easy to descend the slippery slope of desire for personal glory at the expense of a larger vision or cause. This is the trap that appears to have ensnared Jones but never quite got a hold on Nelson.

Illustration #3: The Battle of Copenhagen

In the long struggle with France following the French Revolution, England found it necessary to keep a close watch on the shipping conducted by "neutral" parties. Several of the Baltic countries had grown tired of forceful searches of their merchant ships by the British navy. To deter this infringement upon their commerce by Britain's assertion of its so-called "maritime rights," the countries of Scandinavia, Prussia, and Russia construed the League of Armed Neutrality. By combining their fleets and potentially allying with France, these nations would ensure that the British navy could be challenged for its position as master of the seas. Also, and just as critically, the Baltic had become a major source of supply for Britain's massive navy. Cut off from this source, the British navy could find itself in serious trouble.

By early 1801, the decision was made in London to make a late winter endeavor into the Baltic Sea. If the Royal Navy could first get to Denmark and convince the Danes not to participate in the actions of the League, it could then move further up the Baltic and deal with Russia. If the Danes resisted, they could be dealt with individually, before the thawing of the winter ice allowed the Russian fleet to sail to their aid.

Due to the dual nature of the voyage, part diplomacy and part potential battle, the Admiralty in London decided to send both Admiral Sir Hyde Parker and Vice-Admiral Lord Horatio Nelson as commanders, with Nelson as the junior officer. Perhaps it was thought that Parker's age and discernment might bring a peaceful settlement, but if that failed, the rapacious Nelson could then be unleashed to employ "gunboat diplomacy" to force Britain's position. In essence, that is exactly how things transpired.

Anyone acquainted with the two admirals could have predicted difficulties with the command structure of the expedition. Parker and Nelson could hardly have been more different. Parker had spent many years in charge of a fleet on the very lucrative West Indies station, where prize ships (enemy vessels captured in battle) were rich and plentiful. In the scheme of Royal Navy operations in those days, the value of prizes taken in battle was determined by the Admiralty and then divvied out to the sailors involved in the action. As things went, commanders received the bulk of the money, with a preponderance going to fleet commanders such as Parker.

Having grown extremely rich off his years in the Caribbean, Parker was the quintessential example of a complacent warrior. He had done his time, secured his fame, and made his fortune. Also, to add spice to his comfort, at age sixty-one, Parker had recently married the eighteen-year-old daughter of another sea captain. As Michael Palmer wrote, "With a fortune in one arm and a young wife on the other, Parker's desire to take a winter cruise to the Baltic was somewhat restrained."[4]

Nelson, to the contrary, was hungrier than ever for victory. The architect of the Battle of the Nile, while still revered as a war hero, had returned to London amidst a flurry of self-inflicted scandal. He had become engrossed in a public affair with the wife of the British envoy to Naples. As Nelson, his mistress who was pregnant with his child, and his mistress's husband all arrived in London traveling together, the gossip became thick and surly. Further, Nelson's health was poor. He had lost an arm and complete vision in one eye in previous battles, and his remaining eye was troubling him. Predictably, he also had the final break with his wife. According to Nathan Miller, "It was the low point of Nelson's life."[5] He reached his rendezvous with Parker's fleet ready to blot out his troubles ashore with glory afloat.

Nelson found Parker doing very little to prepare for the campaign. Parker's primary interest appeared to be a birthday party being planned by his young bride. Nelson was furious, and in a famous slip of professionalism he commented, "Consider how nice it must be lying in bed with a young wife, compared to a damned, cold raw wind."[6] Nelson felt the press of time. He knew the British must get to Denmark before the Russian fleet could sail to its aid. Infuriated with Parker's lack of initiative, Nelson took the extraordinary step of writing his superiors in London urging action. Nelson's letter of circumvention did the trick, and the fleet finally set sail. But the relationship between Parker and Nelson hence became as cool as the Baltic Sea to which they were sailing.

It was determined that Copenhagen would be the target where pressure could best be brought against the Danes. Diplomatic efforts had failed to talk Denmark out of the League, so it was obvious Parker and Nelson would have to resort to force, even though England and Denmark were not officially at war.

Feeling righteously determined and having been given plenty of time by Parker's slowness in getting his fleet to the area, the Danes had prepared a stalwart defense of the coast of Copenhagen. The city itself, situated on the eastern shore of the isle of Zealand, protected by dangerous shoals and two islands, was difficult to assault in its own right. To this natural protection, the Danes had lined up a vast array of ships, hulks (old ships that were no longer seaworthy), gun boats, and other various floating defenses. Unlike the French at the Nile, they had anchored these boats close enough to shore that the English would not be able to sail around behind them on the landward side. Additionally, ashore there were forts and batteries of artillery, which were usually much more accurate and damaging than ship's guns because of their stability. To the arriving British, these defenses appeared nearly impregnable, but it was thought that the defenders manning them would not prove nearly as resistant. As the British were about to find out, it would be the exact opposite.

Finally, after taking stock of the city's defenses, the still angry Admiral Parker called his first council of war. Nelson climbed aboard the commander's ship to find the other captains in a state of doubt, very concerned upon finding the Copenhagen defenses stronger than expected. According to Nathan Miller, "Parker was reluctant to send in his ships to attack these powerful batteries and favored blockading...until the allied navies emerged to give battle. That was not Nelson's style. He was for pressing home an attack before the enemy could organize a defense."[7]

Nelson launched into a lengthy diatribe, pacing through Parker's cabin and earnestly goading the other captains to action. According to Miller:

> Parker nervously reminded him [Nelson] that the Danes had some twenty men-of-war and armed hulks in the harbor, along with batteries on the shore, while he had only twelve ships of the line. And what if the Swedes or Russians also showed up? "The more numerous, the better," was Nelson's scornful reply. "I wish they were twice as many."[8]

Since the defenses of Copenhagen were the strongest at the north, Nelson proposed attacking at the softer southern side of the defenses where the enemy would least expect it. Besides, the area was strewn with dangerous shoals, and nobody would expect Nelson to be able to get through. Miller wrote, "But the main thing, Nelson insisted, was to attack—and to attack at once. 'Go by the Sound or by the Belt or anyhow, only lose not an hour,' he declared."[9]

It had been almost seven weeks of delay and deliberation, but Nelson's passionate pleading in Parker's cabin carried the day. The decision was made to attack. However, scouting reports indicated that it would be nearly impossible to pass through the shoals as originally planned, so Parker changed his mind. Access to Copenhagen would be gained through the dangerous northern passage instead. Once through, the fleet could sail to the southern edge of the city and attack as planned. The problem was that the northern passage required sailing within range of guns from both the Danish and Swedish shores. Further, the British possessed no accurate nautical charts of the area showing depths and obstructions. Additionally, a northern wind would be required for the passage and a southern one for the attack. And finally, it was common knowledge in warfare at the time that shore operations held a strong advantage over seaborne attackers. The whole endeavor would be risky. Characteristically, Nelson volunteered to lead it. As Miller wrote, "Parker was only too happy to assign the attack to someone willing to take the risk."[10]

Many of the British ships were too big and heavy to make the northern passage. Also, the whole fleet could not be risked because the Russians had to be dealt with next. So Parker decided to split his forces. The smaller ships with lighter draughts, led by Nelson, would comprise the attacking squadron, and Parker with the heavier ships would provide support and guard against the Russians to the north.

As was his custom, Nelson met with his captains and carefully laid out his battle plans, arranging each ship carefully to balance firepower with the enemy. Then he worked feverishly to bring them into position as the attack began, several of them grounding themselves on the unseen shallows. The battle raged hot and furious, with heavy fire from both sides. As the Danes sustained damage and losses, they reinforced their floating batteries and ships with more men from shore. Surprising the British navy, which had been fighting wars off and on for centuries, the Danish people, who had been at peace for roughly seventy years, fought a courageous and gallant fight.

Pacing the quarterdeck with Nelson throughout the battle was Lieutenant-Colonel Edward Stewart, who wrote:

> Nelson was…walking the starboard side of the quarter-deck; sometimes much animated, and at others heroically fine in his observations. A shot through the mainmast knocked a few splinters about us. He observed to me, with a smile, "It is warm work, and

this day may be the last to any of us at a moment;" and then stopping short at the gangway, he used an expression never to be erased from my memory, and said with emotion, "but mark you, I would not be elsewhere for thousands."[11]

There *was* a commander "elsewhere," however, entirely disengaged from the battle: Parker to the north. Although the wind was favorable for Nelson's attack, that same wind was apparently preventing Parker's ability to engage his portion of the fleet. There are also conflicting reports, which may or may not be true, that a messenger arrived sometime during the battle and boarded Parker's ship with the news that Tsar Paul of Russia, the architect and driving force behind the League of Armed Neutrality, had been assassinated. With this information, the Battle of Copenhagen had likely become unnecessary. And this might have played a part in Parker's subsequent behavior, although neither he nor Nelson ever spoke of it later. At any rate, the battle was at its highest pitch, and the British fleet appeared to be getting the worst of it. Michael A. Palmer wrote:

As Nelson's ships fought their bloody fight, Sir Hyde Parker watched the engagement from the quarterdeck of his flagship....After three hours of battle, the Danish fire appeared undiminished.... Three of Nelson's liners were aground and several ships were flying distress signals. From Parker's perspective, the chaotic scene reeked of disaster.[12]

Dudley Pope termed Parker's subsequent action the "most controversial signal in the history of sea warfare—signal 39, 'to discontinue the engagement.'"[13]

A lieutenant pointed out Parker's signal to Nelson, who was still beside Stewart amidst the thick of the fighting on the quarterdeck. The lieutenant asked if he should hoist a repeat signal to the rest of Nelson's fleet, as was his duty. "No, acknowledge it," Nelson replied. But then after a moment's reflection, Nelson called him back and asked, "Is number 16 [the signal to engage closely] still hoisted [on our own ship]?" The lieutenant answered that it was. "Mind you, keep it so," ordered Nelson. Stewart later recalled Nelson's comments at that moment: "Do you know what's shown on board the Commander-in-Chief, number 39? Why, to leave off action. Leave off action! Now damn me if I do!" Nelson snatched up a looking glass and said, "You know…I have only one eye—and I have a right to be blind sometimes." Then he put the glass to his blind eye. "I really do not see the signal!" (The phrase "turning a blind eye" has been attributed to this scene.) Nelson finished his tirade with, "Damn the signal. Keep mine for close battle flying. That's the way I answer such signals! Nail mine to the mast!"[14]

Parker's signal had flown at the critical high point of the battle. Rear-Admiral Graves, who was also engaged in the fight, wrote:

Sir Hyde made the signal to discontinue the action…supposing that our ships would all be destroyed. But our little Hero gloriously said, "I will not move till we are crowned with victory, or that the Commander-in-Chief sends an officer to order me away." And he was right, for if we had discontinued the action before the enemy struck, we should all have been aground and have been destroyed.

Instead, within an hour of Parker's notorious signal, the Danish fire tapered. The power and discipline of British gunnery was finally winning the battle. When it was obvious the Danes were defeated, Nelson ordered a ceasefire and sent a messenger ashore proposing a truce, staving off further needless destruction.

Figure 2: Nelson at the Battle of Copenhagen

The Danes received nearly 40 percent casualties, with seventeen vessels sunk, burned, or captured. In the second time in three years, Nelson had annihilated an enemy fleet and had accomplished it without losing a single ship of his own. The League of Armed Neutrality subsequently dissolved, and the victory at Copenhagen gave Great Britain a more favorable position to negotiate the upcoming Peace of Amiens with France.

Understanding and Application

Naval expert Admiral Mahan later wrote that the Battle of Copenhagen was "the severest and most doubtful [Nelson] had ever fought."[15] It seems clear from eyewitness accounts and the analysis of experts that the battle could have very readily ended in disaster for the Royal Navy. Instead, the hunger and drive of the attacking commander saw it through. From the moment he joined the fleet until the battle was won, it was Nelson's hunger that drove the expedition. Overcoming the lethargy of a superior commanding officer, ennobling the courage of the fleet's ship captains, convincing the council of war to delay no further and attack, and ignoring a potentially disastrous order at the climax of the battle's intensity, Nelson demonstrated the sustaining force that the hunger of a leader provides.

The contrast in the behavior of Parker as compared to that of Nelson couldn't be more stark. Both were able commanders with significant experience. Both had seen action and had served with distinction. Both were entrusted by the Admiralty in London with an important expedition in the name of their country. But Parker's hesitation and deliberation was incessant, while Nelson's eagerness and aggressiveness could scarcely be contained. What was the difference between these two temperaments as the campaign got underway? Why did two able, worthy commanders behave so differently? The answer, in great part, is that one had grown complacent, and the other, hungrier. Parker was playing not to lose, while Nelson was playing to win. One was on defense, and the other, offense.

As all military commanders know, and as the British saw demonstrated by the Danes's spirited defense of their city, morale is an extremely important factor in conflict. There is a concept called "death ground" that comes from ancient warfare. It is a tactic commanders have used when desperate to get their dispirited troops to fight more effectively, and it occurs by maneuvering one's troops into a position where they either have to win or perish. It closes all the exit doors and allows departure only through the door of victory. This strategy comes from the axiom "When you know you absolutely cannot fail, you won't." Understanding this, a leader must sometimes be willing to maneuver onto a "death ground" in order to maintain a peak level of hunger. Sometimes the vision gets a little blurry. Sometimes the attacks of critics or adversaries wear a leader down. After a long pursuit of a vision, it is common for its allure to wear off slightly and the motivation of the leader to subsequently flag. However, in finding one's self on a death ground, there is no choice but to perform. Hunger will not be a substance wished for but a motivator readily at hand, forcefully pushing the leader forward.

Without doing it intentionally for the purpose of motivation, Nelson had maneuvered himself both physically and figuratively onto a death ground. He had, quite frankly, made a mess of things. His personal life in shambles, he was driven to the one thing he knew best: battle at sea. Having gotten into battle, Nelson found himself on an actual death ground. He and his squadron were literally in a win-or-perish position on the shores of Copenhagen.

This double-death-ground position of Nelson explains his aggressive behavior throughout the expedition. It is the reason he was willing to risk censure and scorn by writing to Parker's superiors and urging them to push the aging admiral into action. It was the force that drove him to motivate and convince the other commanders of the fleet, including Parker, to take the battle to the Danes. And it was the reason behind his ability to decide in the heat of battle, apparently without equivocation, to ignore a direct order and fight on regardless. After the battle, Nelson commented to Stewart, "I have fought contrary to orders, and I shall perhaps be hanged: never mind, let them."[16] Those are the words of a man who knew he had done the right thing. Those are the words of a leader.

Parker, on the other hand, had lost his hunger. Any time a leader loses his or her drive or loses sight of a vision, he or she loses the ability to lead. Unfortunately, the world is full of people who have shone brightly for a moment and led for a while and therefore attained a position of authority. From that position, most people, including themselves, consider them to be a leader. But devoid of hunger, they are nothing of the sort. They become a manager — or less, a figurehead.

Positional leadership is not leadership at all. Some have taken to calling this condition the "Peter Principle," which occurs when one's performance at lower levels of responsibility leads to advancement beyond abilities until one peters out. Regarding Parker, perhaps his contemporary Captain Hotham said it best when he wrote that

Parker was one of those men who "have their characters brought before their brother Officers and who, from the estimation in which they are held in subordinate situations, did not quite fulfill the hopes of what they would be in Chief Commands."[17] In Parker's case, it wasn't his lack of ability that caused him to dither; it was his waning hunger. He had become a man with a title but no vision. His men knew it, and after the Battle of Copenhagen, his superiors knew it too. They recalled Parker from the fleet and put Nelson in charge.

Roy and Lesley Adkins wrote of Parker's behavior at the Battle of Copenhagen, "It was inexplicable to Nelson and his officers at the time, and remains so today."[18] This might not be entirely true. A large part of Parker's behavior is explainable by his lack of hunger. It's the substance of leadership, and Parker had lost it.

Illustration #4: English Navy versus French Navy in the Seven Years' War

The Seven Years' War between England and France (called the French and Indian War in America) has been called by many the first "world war." In essence, it was a contest between the world's two predominant super powers at the time, each striving for world dominance through the conquest of colonial territories and the control of the seas necessary to harvest the wealth those colonies could provide. Great Britain, an island country, depended heavily on its overseas colonies for trade and income, while

France was just as hungry to secure its lucrative colonies and gain dominance over its archrival.

There was a key difference between the two adversaries, however. France, a mainland European country with a large, rich territory of its own and sea ports in the English Channel, the Atlantic, and the Mediterranean, was well-endowed for dominance. Great Britain, on the other hand, as a small island country, was entirely dependent upon waterborne commerce for its health and survival.

The English had recognized this for quite some time. In fact, a large faction developed in the British Parliament that was entirely opposed to land-based wars and urged Britain to stick to its strength: the Royal Navy. This faction came to be called the "blue water school." The founder of that line of thinking, Jonathan Swift, wrote that making war upon the sea was founded upon "all the maxims of British policy, the sea being the element where we might most probably carry on the war with any advantage to our selves." As early as 1718, a British writer understood the truth of Britain's perilous position in world geopolitics, stating that it was "the vastness and extensiveness of our trade that made Britain the most considerable of any nation in the world." A tiny island nation had risen to rival the strongest nations in Europe on the back of its navy.[19]

Perhaps no one understood the foundation of the strength of Great Britain any better than the most extraordinary politician in England at the time, William Pitt. At first, as a young member of Parliament, Pitt seemed to focus on the power of British trade around the globe, saying

"When trade is at stake, it is your last entrenchment; you must defend it or perish." Pitt's strategy evolved, and according to Arthur Herman:

> Pitt would turn the standard formula for sea power and trade inside out. Instead of seeing the navy as a weapon for getting and defending overseas empire, he saw overseas empire as a tool for the navy, giving it the bases it needed to defend British mercantile interests and to increase its own global reach.[20]

The secret to the strength of Great Britain was not in the outdated concept of global mercantilism but in the strength of its battle fleets. Global commerce was no longer the darling of the country, but rather the Royal Navy was. The more far-flung and dispersed the British empire, the more the seas allowed the Royal Navy to leverage its dominance, showing up in remote corners of the world to enforce its policies. The seas did not divide the world — they connected it. And the vehicle that best utilized that connection was the Royal Navy. This line of thinking turned Britain's apparent weakness — its radically dispersed colonial holdings — into its greatest strength.

This change in understanding of Britain's position in the balance of world power was important because it brought it into direct conflict with France. By the time of Louis XV, France had become an extremely militarized society. In an odd period of sociology, difficult for those of us in the twenty-first century to understand, commerce and the making of money through enterprise were looked down upon by most in France. A person was born into a position in society, and opportunities for advancement to those not of high birth were virtually nonexistent. Involvement in the church was confined to a select few. For most, the only remaining opportunity for glory and advancement in mid-eighteenth-century France was through the military. One could most readily climb up through society by descending into the depths of war. Armed with such a martial populace, France sought to be the preeminent power in Europe and to tighten its grip on overseas holdings.

Thus were positioned the world's two dominant powers.

When the Seven Years' War began between the two nations, both sides were ramping up their navies, building ships, and training officers at a fiendish pace. The war, taking place as much on land as at sea, went well for the French until the year 1759. It was then that the tide turned, and it did so upon the hinges provided by the British Royal Navy.

Amphibious operations are those coordinating navy and ground troops. In 1759, these began to succeed for the British. Also, the Royal Navy was instrumental in delivering supplies to landed troops and stopping supply and reinforcements from the French navy as well as winning victories against French ships at sea. Strategic to its success was the development of the close blockade of major French harbors. This neutralized large percentages of the French fleet by trapping them in their own harbors and not allowing them to sail out, lest they be attacked by a waiting British squadron.

France was defeated at several battles in India in which the Royal Navy played a key role. Then Quebec in Canada fell, due in large part to the transport and firepower of British ships. Senegal, the hub of the French slave trade on the coast of West Africa, also fell to the English. At a sea battle off Lagos Bay, Portugal, the Royal Navy defeated a French fleet and severely hampered French plans for an invasion of England. Those plans effectively came to an end when the Royal Navy won a major victory at Quiberon Bay, destroying a large part of the French fleet trying to escape blockade.

The English appeared to be victorious everywhere. In contrast, the French were losing their overseas possessions at an alarming rate. Much of it came down to the contest between the two navies. Even though both countries had been building new fighting ships continuously since before the war, the English were more committed to their navy and had gained a sizeable advantage. By 1758, the British had over three times as many ships as the French. As Frank McLynn wrote, "The mighty French fleet had been humiliated and...never put to sea again during the Seven Years War."[21]

Understanding and Application

The Seven Years' War was a demonstration that even a tiny island nation could dominate the world, depending of course on the strength of its navy. Great Britain seemed to understand this clearly and focused on building and maintaining the world's largest, most effective and dominant naval power. The French, in contrast, were divided between building and sustaining both land and naval forces. As the war dragged on, the French navy received increasing neglect at the hands of its monarch.

Hunger is the secret to effective leadership. It initiates a leader's actions and sustains them through to completion. As we see clearly in the contest between the two navies in the Seven Years' War, hunger affects entire institutions, not just individuals. It was the hunger of the British Royal Navy that made the difference in the war. Time and again, the Royal Navy showed more discipline and skill in battle. The naval administration of Great Britain showed a higher level of commitment to sea power than did its counterparts. It seemed to be the understanding of everyone in Great Britain, right down to the humblest commoner, that control of the seas was critical to their survival. In contrast, the navy was just a portion of France's martial force.

In a way, Great Britain was on a "death ground." It knew that it either floated a strong and effective navy, or it would perish. In such a position, the entire country developed a culture of hunger to dominate the seas. From way back in its history, its leaders had also demonstrated such a hunger, and William Pitt was the current embodiment of that hunger at the level of national leadership. The entire country was committed to the sacrifices and the resources required to field and maintain such a large and powerful navy.

This example illustrates a concept called *collective hunger* that can develop in organizations. It is a hunger that resonates from the leaders. This hunger is extremely critical to effective leadership because it is the force that impels individuals and institutions through all the necessary steps between the initial disdain for the status quo and eventual success. It is this hunger that compels people to sacrifice, to stay the course, to innovate, and to strive against resistance. It is this hunger that motivates both individuals and organizations to finish well what they've begun. As President Calvin Coolidge is attributed with saying:

Nothing in the World can take the place of persistence. Talent will not; nothing is more common than unsuccessful men with talent. Genius will not; unrewarded genius is almost a proverb. Education will not; the world is full of educated derelicts. Persistence and determination alone are omnipotent. The slogan, "press on" has solved and always will solve the problems of the human race.[22]

Hunger is the substance that compels a leader or an organization to "press on."

In a contest between two parties, the best results will almost always go the hungriest. Fighting for survival gives one a decided advantage. A leader who *can't* lose *won't*. Wise leaders quickly identify their nonnegotiables. Further, if a clear understanding of the situation can be communicated throughout the organization, a collective hunger will develop. This becomes a tremendous advantage.

Summary

Hunger is the fuel of leadership greatness. Leaders are driven by a hunger to assault the status quo and pursue a vision of something better. Hunger initiates the actions of a leader and sustains and inspires the leader until the objective is accomplished.

Hunger is actually a discipline. It is like a muscle that must be used on a regular basis in order to remain strong. Understanding the crucial role hunger plays in leadership, wise leaders seek ways to stoke the flames of their hunger. In many cases, circumstances themselves provide the necessary motivation. In a "death ground" situation, the leader either performs or faces ruin. But leaders don't have to wait for circumstances to arise; they can maneuver themselves into such a position on purpose. Further, leaders should always be searching for sources of hunger — such as reminding themselves of material rewards or recognition, looking for respect from mentors and peers, and most important, keeping themselves mindful of the cause for which they fight and the purpose for which they strive.

Maintaining the hunger that started the quest throughout the ups and downs of the journey is the key to leaders finishing well — and even finishing at all. Hunger sustains. Hunger inspires. It unites. It influences. Without hunger, leaders can't lead, and they won't be followed. With hunger, almost anything is possible. Wise leaders court hunger like a muse, and they summon her continuously. Complacency, arrogance, malevolence, apathy, and comfort can easily chase her away. Leaders who are able to stay the course are able to both sustain hunger and keep these dangerous temptations at bay.

CHAPTER THREE

The Lesson of Initiative

Leadership Principle:

One trait common to all leaders is initiative. Leaders don't have to be told to do something. They don't need managers above them. They don't wait for all the lights to turn green before departing on a trip. Leaders don't waste time waiting and wondering if they should act. They take responsibility and take action. There is an old line that there are three types of people in the world: those who make things happen, those who watch things happen, and those who wonder what happened. Leaders are the ones in the first group making things happen.

A component in initiative is the courage to act. Another is decisiveness. Leaders display a willingness toward action, seeing what needs to be done and doing it without delay.

Initiative is not to be confused with recklessness. Instead, it is a mixture of a spirit of enterprise, courage, and competent decisiveness.

Illustration #1: Edward Pellew and the *Indefatigable*

The French Revolution of 1789 had begun on the high ideals of Liberty, Equality, and Fraternity but had descended into the Reign of Terror and the guillotine. Eventually, the more moderate Directory took over the affairs of the country and set its sights on dominance and dominion.

In its war with Great Britain, France had seen momentum swing its way. By 1795, it had recaptured islands in the Caribbean that it had previously lost to the English, and it had secured three of its borders in mainland Europe. Spain then decided to sign on as an ally of France. With this development, the Royal Navy's presence in the Mediterranean was threatened, and it was forced to withdraw from those waters for the first time in ages. This withdrawal forced Britain's one remaining ally, Austria, to give up hope and sue for peace with France. Now Great Britain stood alone.

According to Arthur Herman:

The Directory sensed final victory. One more blow directed at Britain might do it. But how to bring its invincible army to bear against an enemy protected by the English Channel — and the fleet at Spithead? This was the problem that would perplex and baffle France's best military minds, including Bonaparte, for more than a decade. It equally baffled Hitler and his generals in 1940. Philip II and Louis XIV had each failed to find the solution, even when they enjoyed naval superiority. There was England with its puny army, its exposed beaches, its capital vulnerable to attack: the last barrier to complete French domination of Europe. Yet it would not give way.[1]

So the French struck upon an idea to attack the Irish coast, hoping to take advantage of rebel sentiment there and gather an army of Irishmen to assist them in their conquest of England.

Out of the port of Brest, a French squadron of seventeen ships of the line loaded with 15,000 soldiers was dispatched for the attack. The British had been maintaining a blockade of the harbor, keeping watch on the French fleet and trying to keep it bottled up in port. The weather, though, had grown harsh, and the ships of the Royal Navy had been blown far off station and out into the Atlantic — except for one.

The *Indefatigable* was only a frigate, not a full-size line of battle ship but of the class of faster, lighter ships meant for speed and reconnaissance. Through the foulest weather he could ever remember, Captain Edward Pellew had heroically managed to remain on his station. He alone was there to spot the large French fleet making its way out to sea.

Realizing that there was not enough time to sail out in the Atlantic and alert the British squadron, Pellew seized the initiative. In the darkness of the night and in a torrential downpour, he immediately sailed his tiny frigate directly into the middle of the French fleet. As the enormous French battle ships labored to maneuver their way around the rocks and shoals at the mouth of the harbor, Pellew and the *Indefatigable* deftly sailed amongst them, firing off guns and flares, attempting to imitate the French signals and cause confusion. Pellew's tiny ship was everywhere. The result was chaos. One of the large battleships, the *Séduisant*, ran onto the rocks. Several others were scattered out into the Atlantic, including the one carrying the French admiral and general.

Pellew had acted courageously and decisively and had demonstrated ingenuity all at the same time. His efforts had caused just enough of a delay. The French fleet took time to reassemble, and once it did, the weather had turned into an ice storm. The winds were contrary to a landing on the shores of Ireland, and the invasion had to be called off. The initiative of one leader and his crew had made the difference.

Understanding and Application

Captain Pellew didn't deliberate in the face of a challenge. He didn't need to get orders before acting. He saw what needed to be done, exhibited great courage and ingenuity, and took responsibility for getting results. And as we have seen before, one leader's initiative made an enormous difference.

Those who deliberate, dilly-dally, hesitate, ponder, get bogged down in analysis, or have to be sure everything is perfect before taking action might do a very good job at what they do; they just don't get much of it accomplished. They have beautifully detailed goals but don't ever seem to hit them, and they have all kinds of theoretical knowledge about how things are going to work out for them once everything is perfectly situated to make an attempt.

It is almost always the go-getters who become the biggest leaders. To lead implies action, and all leaders are people of action. There are usually people who have more talent, more time, more connections, more means, and more information than the leader, but the leader emerges to influence events because he or she takes action while others hesitate. This is not to imply that all leaders are reckless or reactive—though some may be—but rather that leaders err on the side of decisiveness. Over time, the tendency toward action builds ability, so deficiencies of talent or means are eventually overcome.

In short, action over time breeds effectiveness.

Illustration #2: Commander Oliver Perry at the Battle of Lake Erie

After the Treaty of Paris was signed in 1783, ending the War for Independence, conflict with Britain continued to aggravate the fledgling United States. After suffering trade restrictions imposed by the British, the impressment of American merchant sailors into the Royal Navy, insults to America's national honor, and other hostilities, the United States, under President James Madison, declared war against Britain in 1812. In many ways, the War of 1812 put an official stamp on America's independence and finally ended British hostilities.

When war broke out, the British, who already had a small force of warships on Lake Erie, immediately seized control of the lake. At the age of twenty-seven and at his own request, Oliver Hazard Perry was given command of the US naval force on Lake Erie. He was charged with building a fleet on Presque Isle Bay to take on the British. He arrived on the island in early March of 1813.

Under his supervision, the American squadron was almost complete by mid-July, though it was not yet fully manned. The British, under Commander Robert Barclay, blockaded Presque Isle for ten days. Fortunately, a sandbar across the harbor prevented them from sailing in and attacking the new American ships. Due to a shortage of supplies and bad weather, the British were forced to lift the blockade. Seeing the British leave, Perry immediately began moving his vessels across the sandbar into the open sea. Four days later, Barclay returned to find that Perry had nearly completed the task. Facing a line of gunboats ready for action, Barclay withdrew. Perry then set upon the task to man his ships with volunteers.

Shortly after, Perry was able to turn the tables on Barclay and establish a blockade against the British, who quickly ran out of supplies. Barclay was forced to put out to sea and seek battle with Perry.

On the morning of September 10, the Americans saw Barclay's ships heading for them under a light wind. Both squadrons were formed in the line of battle, with their heaviest ships near the center of the line. Perry commanded his flagship, the *Lawrence*, while Lieutenant Jesse Elliot commanded the next heaviest ship, the *Niagara*. Perry's hope was to get these two largest ships into cannon range quickly, but the light wind impeded their progress. The *Lawrence* was battered by long guns mounted in Barclay's *Detroit* for twenty minutes before being able to fire back. When his ship was finally able to fire, Perry was frustrated again when his gunners overloaded the cannons, thus making their fire far less effective.

Meanwhile, Elliot hung back in the *Niagara*, astern of the *Lawrence* and far out of effective cannon range. It wasn't long before Perry's ship was demolished. Four-fifths of his crew were killed or wounded. When his last gun was destroyed, Perry jumped aboard a rowboat and rowed half a mile through heavy gunfire to the *Niagara* while the *Lawrence* was surrendered. The British expected the *Niagara* to lead the remaining American ships in retreat. But rather than retreating, Perry commandeered Elliot's ship and dispatched him to bring the other American ships into closer action. After taking over, he immediately steered the *Niagara* at Barclay's damaged ships.

In a move reminiscent of Lord Nelson, whom he had studied zealously, Perry broke through the British line and began raking Barclay's ships with broadsides. The British flagships surrendered at 3:00 p.m. Their smaller vessels tried to flee but were overtaken and also surrendered. Although he paid a terrible price, Perry won the battle through initiative and decisiveness.

Illustration #3: Sir Edward Hawke's Blockade of Brest

Thirty-six years before Captain Pellew made his courageous interference with a French squadron escaping out of the harbor of Brest, another English captain was in a similar position. The year was 1759, the pivotal year in the Seven Years' War between France and Great Britain.

Britain's Royal Navy had grown in size and professionalism. With a clear understanding that its objective was to rule the seas, the Royal Navy had taken a terrible toll on French shipping and commerce. The English had been so successful that France was increasingly cut off from its colonies in Canada and the West Indies. It was feared, correctly as it turned out, that without a turn in fortunes, Canada would be lost to the English. Just as they had previously, and would again decades later, the French concluded that their best hope was an invasion of England. Three years earlier, the mere assembling of a force to invade England had kept most of the Royal Navy close to home in the English Channel for protection, freeing French ships to sail where they pleased. Perhaps the same result would occur again, allowing French fleets to supply the beleaguered soldiers in Canada. Preparations for the invasion moved forward, with major activity taking place in the harbors of Brest and Quiberon Bay, France.

Admiral Sir Edward Hawke was in command of Britain's Western Squadron, which had responsibility for the protection of the English coast. Hawke had orders to cruise to Brest within fourteen days, check on French invasion preparations there, and return to a home port for reprovisioning. When Hawke got to Brest, however, he was confronted with eleven full-size battle ships appearing capable of sailing out of the harbor at any time. He immediately decided to countermand his orders and began a close blockade of the harbor instead.

Blockading an enemy harbor was not new. Amassing a fleet of ships off the coast of an enemy port was an effective strategy because the ships at sea had a distinct advantage over those that would try to come out of the port and engage in battle. With the slow speeds of sailing ships, their reliance on wind and its direction, and the large amount of space required to bring a fleet of ships into proper formation for battle, any fleet emerging from port into the waiting ships of an enemy blockade would be in for utter destruction.

Hawke, however, took the concept of close blockade a step further than usual. Already low on provisions, he knew he and his fleet could not last long outside the enemy port. Water was in short supply, and it wouldn't be long before all the other victuals would run out. So he initiated a system of resupply at sea. What sounds so obvious and simple to modern ears was actually quite revolutionary at the time. Hawke sent ships back to English ports to obtain supplies and had them rendezvous with various ships under his command out to sea. The ships on blockade duty would then either go out in small groups to meet those ships for resupply or would have supplies brought to them. This idea had been considered before and even tried in limited ways but had never met with much success or favor with commanders. With Hawke, however, an aggressive and strategic commander, the concept worked remarkably well.

Hawke's close blockade effectively took the French fleet at Brest entirely out of the plans for invasion. That was not all. With the English ships on constant duty at sea, keeping watch over the trapped French ships, the morale of English sailors soared, while that of the French plummeted. There was just something intimidating and demoralizing about being trapped at harbor, watching an enemy off shore show its flag every day, baiting you to come out and fight. Additionally, the English used their time to hone their skills, getting actual sailing time twenty-four hours a day, seven days a week, and practicing their gunnery. The French were growing rusty, while the English were growing strong. Additionally, the French port was effectively blocked off from receiving any waterborne commerce or supplies. The large French fleet instead had to be sustained with expensive and slow overland operations.

According to author Peter Padfield, "This relentless grip on the enemy fleet base formed the cornerstone of a series of victories that year which established Great Britain as the final winner at sea and across the seas; as such it ranks among the most decisive naval campaigns in world history."[2] And it all began with Hawke's decision to cast aside his orders and pioneer the idea of a sustainable close blockade.

Finally, frustrated by the effectiveness of Hawke's blockade, the French fleet made an ill-advised escape when winds were favorable to them and had blown the British out into the Atlantic. It was the kind of move for which Hawke had been hoping. With incredible decisiveness and almost reckless abandon, he pursued the French south as they fled into Quiberon Bay. With terrible weather, dangerous rocks all around, and the day's light fading quickly, Hawke charged ahead for the attack. Padfield wrote:

> The scene was the grandest in the long history of Anglo-French wars: under low skies darkened with lines of squalls, the two fleets drove down the spume-lathered swell from the Atlantic, ships heeling wildly as the wind gusted up and shifted a degree or so, tiers of canvas whipped taut, topmasts, t'gallants and slender stunsail booms quivering with the strain, weather rigging stretched bartight, timber groaning, water torn through the head gratings as the bows plunged, pressing out wide patterns of foam, the sea surging swiftly down the sides....
>
> Quiberon Bay...put an end to [King] Louis XV's invasion plans and to his battle fleet, which ceased to exist as an effective force. The victory was a natural outcome of the close blockade which had preceded it.[3]

Hawke's victory at Quiberon Bay was total. Speaking of J. Creswell's astute observation regarding the victory, Padfield wrote, "It has been observed, with justice, that 'no more courageous decision in the handling of a navy's main battle fleet has ever been taken.'"[4]

Understanding and Application

Being a sea captain in the nineteenth century was a picture of loneliness. Far out to sea, separated from superiors and all lines of communication, with orders that were usually months old, these men were forced to rely on their own judgment. There was no one else on scene to guide their actions or concur with their decisions. It is a beautiful picture of leadership.

Leaders know that their very calling requires decision, courage, and action. Often, leaders are confronted with facts they don't like, circumstances that put them at peril, and adversaries that mean them harm. Further, there will not always be time to gather adequate intelligence before taking action, and the odds will not always be in a leader's favor. A leader takes stock of a situation, confronts brutal reality without denial or panic, and calculates the best plan of action.

Since time is almost always of the essence, leaders are normally faced with making decisions on their own. Usually there just isn't time for consultations and committee approval. Then, once the leader makes a decision and takes action accordingly, he or she takes great pains to make the decision into a correct one. As one lawyer stated,

"I have never seen a case I couldn't win, if properly handled, and I've never seen a case I couldn't lose, either." A true leader makes a decision and then works to make the decision right.

In the course of "making it right," leaders are often forced to improvise. The story of Perry leaving his ship and commandeering another American ship to continue the battle is a study in bold initiative and courageous persistence. While his lieutenant held back, Perry pushed forward. Then, rather than waiting for reinforcements to relieve him, he went back and brought reinforcements into battle with him. In the heat of battle, he did whatever was necessary to ensure victory.

Hawke's courageous decision to countermand his orders and blockade Brest, which he was unprepared to do, was bold enough. But then creating a way to sustain his decision proved to be the masterstroke. It not only gave him an enormous strategic advantage over his enemy but ultimately caused one of the most devastating battles in naval history. It should also be noted that Hawke's innovation became a new standard of operation for the Royal Navy and a major weapon against the French in its own right. The impact of Hawke's methods of resupply at sea and resulting long-term close blockade were used extensively in the later Napoleonic Wars to enormous effect.

Action and the habit of initiative, in addition to developing a leader's effectiveness, also tend to foster creativity. Innovation in the face of adversity is a key component in the initiative required of a leader. Where many people, when confronted with difficult circumstances, hesitate, gather more information, and seek to ask superiors for advice and assistance, leaders enact creative solutions and take action. If there isn't a ready-made solution, they invent one. What others may perceive as a gamble, leaders understand to be merely a calculated risk. In the face of superior odds, a leader must have the courage to innovate.

Illustration #4: Nelson's "Patent Bridge for Boarding First Rates"

France and its allies planned an invasion of Ireland in 1797. It was an old strategy for attacking the British from their weak underbelly. Admiral Sir John Jervis of the Royal Navy was in charge of the Mediterranean squadron and was trying to intercept a large Spanish squadron he thought to be in the area of the southern tip of Portugal, off Cape St. Vincent. Jervis had fifteen sail of the line.

They caught up with the Spanish fleet in the early morning hours of February 14. It wasn't until dawn that the British realized that they were outnumbered nearly two to one. One sailor recorded a conversation with Jervis as one Spanish ship after another was revealed:

"There are eight sail of the line, Sir John."
"Very well, sir."
"There are twenty sail of the line, Sir John."
"Very well, sir."
"There are twenty-five sail of the line, Sir John."
"Very well, sir."

"There are twenty-seven sail of the line, Sir John."

"Enough, sir, no more of that; the die is cast, and if there are fifty sail I will go through them."[5]

The fleet the British faced that day represented the main body of the Spanish navy. Jervis realized that the situation would only get worse if the Spanish were to join up with the French. If Jervis could inflict enough damage, the Spanish would be helpless to join France in the attack of Ireland.

Flushed with the spirit of their commander, the British fleet sailed directly at the Spanish to bring on a full engagement. The Spanish line was not formed well, and large gaps opened up between clusters of their ships, particularly between their center and rear. Jervis decided to exploit the sloppy sailing of his enemy and signaled to his fleet to sail right for the gap. The signal flags, and the commands they represented, were a little confusing. Recent changes had been made to the standard signal book, and Jervis's intentions were not entirely clear to his ship captains. The lead ships in Jervis's fleet, called the "van," managed to break through the enemy line. Then Jervis gave the signal for his fleet to tack in succession (turn one after the other). Several did, but then the wind changed.

Suddenly, the ships at the rear of the Spanish line were able to bear down on the ships at the front of Jervis's fleet. With the change in the wind, the ships in the center and rear of Jervis's fleet had to quickly change direction, or else they would be cut off from the lead British ships; the wind was pushing them farther and farther away. This would, in effect, split his forces the way he had just split the Spanish and could be devastating to his fleet, stranding the five ships of his van alone against nineteen enemy ships. The best way for the center and rear of Jervis's fleet to maneuver into position was to "wear," which means to turn their bows through the wind instead of away from it. But given the position of his ships, no signal in the signal book would have made sense to the other commanders. Further complications arose from the fact that the ship at the very rear of Jervis's line was over three miles away, and through the battle smoke, it would be impossible to see any signal flag he flew from the mast anyway. The frigates that would usually relay such signals had to stand off at a distance because of the way Jervis's fleet had sailed down the opposite side of the enemy. In short, Jervis was limited by his communication technology.

Jervis decided to signal to the lead ship of his rear division, just four ships behind him, hoping that if it made a maneuver, the captains of the ships behind it would understand that they were to follow suit. The ship, already damaged from the fighting, failed to react to the signal and continued sailing in the same direction. Jervis and his fleet were in deep peril.

According to Michael A. Palmer:

Only one ship to Jervis's rear did respond to the signal—the *Captain* 74, commanded by Horatio Nelson. Nelson knew the signal book, and its limitations, as well as anyone in the fleet. He recognized in Jervis's signal evidence of a "well-arranged design" and, in an extraordinary display of initiative, acted accordingly. While several of Nelson's fellow captains witnessed his maneuver, not one followed his example.[6]

Nelson charged into the fray, filling the weakest part of the British position, engaging three enemy ships at once. One of the ships was the four-decker *Santísima Trinidad*, the largest warship afloat, and the other two were enormous three-deckers, the *San Nicolas* and *San Josef*. To say that Nelson in the *Captain* was outgunned would be a wild understatement.

Finally, one of Nelson's close friends, Captain Collingwood of the *Excellent*, responded to another signal from Jervis and sailed directly to Nelson's aid. It was almost too late, as Nelson's ship was nearly torn to shreds. Then, in all the confusion caused by the arrival of Collingwood, the two Spanish triple-deckers smashed into each other and became entangled. Knowing that his wheel and rigging were shot off and that the *Captain* would be impossible to sail away, Nelson made a quick decision: he ordered his first officer, Captain Miller, to sail closer to the Spanish ship with the intention of boarding her. When the ships collided, Miller stepped forward to lead his men. "No Miller," Nelson said, drawing his sword, "I must have that honour."[7] The British sailors boarded the *San Nicolas* through the captain's cabin, with Spanish officers pouring fire through the cabin door. With Nelson in the lead, the British marines pried open the door and shot their way out to the quarterdeck.

While the British hauled down *San Nicolas's* colors, soldiers from the *San Josef* fired on them. In a split-second decision, Nelson ordered his men to board the *San Josef* from the *San Nicolas*, shouting, "Boarders away!" Within seconds, a horde of marines had stormed *San Josef's* deck. By the time Nelson boarded, the Spanish were surrendering. The Spanish fleet soon retreated, and the battle was won.

After the battle, Nelson boarded the *Victory* where Jervis greeted him with a warm embrace. When Captain Robert Calder groused that Nelson had disobeyed orders, Jervis snapped back, "It certainly was so, and if ever you commit such a breach of your orders, I will forgive you also."[8] Nelson wrote to his wife that "every man, from the highest to the lowest in the fleet"[9] praised him. Common seamen asked to shake his hand, while officers, with no small amount of admiration, joked about Nelson's "Patent Bridge for Boarding First-Rates."[10]

Figure 3: "Nelson's Patent Bridge for Boarding First Rates" at the Battle of Cape St. Vincent, 14th February, 1797 by Thomas Buttersworth

Only four of the Spanish ships were captured in the entire engagement—and two of them by Nelson. Even though much of the Spanish fleet got away, the Battle of Cape St. Vincent likely saved Ireland from invasion and definitely had major political ramifications back home. It also demonstrated that England had a leader who wasn't afraid to take initiative when necessary, understanding the intentions of a superior and doing what needed to be done without explicit instructions.

Understanding and Application

A leader sees what needs to be done and does it, even if sometimes it may appear to be directly opposite of what is expected. In the case of Nelson at Cape St. Vincent, he actually had to act in apparent contradiction to orders to take the initiative his admiral expected of him.

What separates a leader from the rest is not only his ability to see what needs to be done but his unhesitating execution of it, even while others watch or deliberate. As Palmer wrote, "Nelson had not been the only commander in the rear who recognized what needed to be done; he had simply been the only one willing to take the professional risk to react."[11]

Nelson's actions at Cape St. Vincent demonstrate another aspect of initiative: courage. In all cases, the requirements of a leader to take initiative, be action-oriented, and innovate when necessary all involve courage. A leader without courage is not a leader at all. Courage, it should be noted, is not action instead of fear but rather action *in spite* of fear. Leaders feel just as much trepidation as others, but they are able to muster the courage to press on anyway. This is why when the going gets tough, people look for a leader. They want someone with the courage to confront challenges and hit obstacles head on, thereby inspiring them to do the same. A leader absolutely must be courageous. As John C. Maxwell wrote, "A leader is one who knows the way, goes the way, and shows the way."[12] This cannot be done without courage.

In the case of Nelson at Cape St. Vincent, we see physical courage displayed as he led his ship into a near suicidal position. Then he demonstrated it again, and perhaps even more so, when he personally led the dangerous mission of boarding an enemy vessel and then, incredibly, a second one as well! This is courage in one of its highest forms.

It may be tempting for some to analyze the actions of Nelson and conclude that his courage was not much more than recklessness. But Nelson didn't take chances for which he hadn't calculated outcomes. He was careful not to risk his sailors until he had carefully briefed them on their duties and the strategy for engagement. In his larger fleet actions, he was diligent in spending time with his captains, teaching them all about his philosophy for battle so that when the time came, they would each be prepared at the highest level. When Nelson led the boarding party across the gunwales of the second enemy ship at Cape St. Vincent, it was in large part an act of self-defense. Nelson's actions at the Battle of Cape St. Vincent were not recklessness but bravery. He saw what needed to be done and did it unhesitatingly.

Leaders are those who take initiative by spotting gaps and filling them, without direction, without hesitation, and without regard for their own well-being. Leaders can sometimes take the concept of initiative too far, however, and slip into recklessness, which serves no one and actually becomes a disservice to those in the leader's charge.

Illustration #5: USS *Chesapeake* versus HMS *Shannon*

In the War of 1812, the new United States found itself grappling with its former sovereign and was extremely outmatched. Great Britain had long been master of the seas, boasting the world's largest and most successful navy, with a rich tradition of victory and esprit de corps. In contrast, the United States had a small fleet of gunships (which were strictly for coastal protection and not even very effective in their purpose), six newly-constructed frigates, and little else in its "navy." Surprisingly though, the Americans had started the war with several ship-to-ship victories—five in all—in which their new-design large frigates had repeatedly defeated British ships at their own game.

The following year, the captain of one of the American frigates, the *Chesapeake*, fell sick, as did several of his key officers. This only added to the stigma of the *Chesapeake* being an unlucky ship. A new captain and officers were named. James Lawrence was the newest officer on the eligibility list for command of one of the coveted frigates. In a previous command aboard a smaller American vessel, he had challenged the captain of a British war ship to a ship-to-ship duel. When the British commander refused, stating that such an action would violate his orders, Lawrence was verbal in his denouncement of the man as a coward. This portion of Lawrence's past would soon nearly repeat itself.

The British ship *Shannon,* also a frigate, was commanded by one of the English Royal Navy's most able captains: Philip Broke. As Ian W. Toll wrote:

In the post-Nelson, post-Trafalgar era of unquestioned naval supremacy, when the remnants of France's navy were mostly caged in its harbors, and occasions to fire a shot in anger were few and far between, the Royal Navy's overall standards of gunnery and readiness had declined. The *Shannon* was an exception. Captain Broke was a zealous advocate of daily gun drills. *Shannon* was as ready for battle as any frigate had ever been, and Captain Broke wanted the opportunity to prove it.[13]

Broke was on duty off the coast of Boston Harbor, given the task of either bottling the new American frigates in harbor or destroying them if they should come out. In line with this objective, Broke decided to challenge the American frigates to leave the harbor and engage in a fair, ship-to-ship duel. He sent his message verbally to shore via several smaller passing boats. At the time, the two American captains on station had refused and then later escaped out of harbor as ordered and proceeded to sea. As Lawrence took over command of the *Chesapeake*, however, Broke tried again, this time issuing a formal written challenge. The letter, although preserved for history, never made it into Lawrence's hands. History is silent as to whether Lawrence learned of the challenge by other means.

Lawrence had orders to get his ship out of harbor and avoid engagement with the Royal Navy's ships watching diligently off the coast. He was then to focus on attacking British commerce vessels and troop transports reinforcing England's positions in Canada. The best naval strategy for the United States was to inflict economic damage on England's merchant shipping. Although the surprising victories by America's frigates the past year had electrified the nation and provided the only bright spot in the war so far, they actually did very little to procure an end to the conflict. Ship-to-ship battles were actually much more strategic for the British. Since the United States had but a small number of vessels, ship-to-ship battles were extremely risky because any loss or damage would reduce an already miniscule navy. Additionally, the time and cost of building the new, larger-style American frigates had been enormous. In terms of timeliness for this war, the existing ones were irreplaceable. Finally, the new frigate designs were revolutionary and very effective, and as such, a strategic advantage. Capture by the enemy would provide the British with a master upon which to craft their own. In short, Lawrence's orders were to get loose in the large Atlantic and wreak havoc upon British commerce but in no way put his valuable frigate at risk of capture or destruction.

In command of his new ship a mere two weeks, with over half of his officers and a quarter of his crew also new, many having never fired the ship's guns, Lawrence hurried out to sea. He didn't wait for weather that would allow him to slip out of harbor unnoticed but rather sailed in broad daylight toward a direct engagement with the *Shannon*. We know this because Lawrence wrote two letters explaining his intentions as he rounded the entrance to the harbor.

The *Shannon* sailed out to sea and awaited its prey. Followed for a while by well-wishers and civilian admirers, the *Chesapeake* finally out-sailed them and made its way into battle position. First one large gun fired, followed by another and another until the deafening sound cascaded into one continuous thunder, both ships giving full broadsides as quickly as possible. Small arms fire from the tops of the *Shannon's* mastheads was also extremely lethal. Damage to both sides was immense, but within the first two minutes, more than 100 of the 150 men stationed on the exposed deck of the *Chesapeake* were dead, including most of its officers. Also, three helmsmen in a row were killed aboard the *Chesapeake* in rapid succession, and its wheel was blasted apart and became entirely unusable. With severely damaged rigging and no immediate way to provide steerage, the *Chesapeake* at first turned its stern to the *Shannon*, allowing devastating raking fire to travel down its entire length. Then, with head sails ruined and few men left to give orders, the *Chesapeake* actually sailed backwards toward the *Shannon*. The raking fire continued until not a man was standing aboard the *Chesapeake's* quarterdeck. When the two ships collided, there was no one to give the order to board the *Shannon*, the last hope the disabled *Chesapeake* would have had for victory.

Dragged below deck and fighting for his life, the wounded Lawrence famously said, "Don't give up the ship."[14] At one point, he even tried to order his men to blow the ship up to keep it from falling into British hands. It was an order for suicide that wasn't followed, and it was too late for even desperate measures anyway. Captain Broke and a band of less than thirty men were all that boarded the *Chesapeake* and finalized its capture. The entire engagement had lasted less than fifteen minutes! It was one of the bloodiest and most convincing victories in the history of naval war. According to Toll, "Broke had done it; the doubts could be laughed away; the Royal Navy's honor was saved, and the world that had been turned upside down, in those few disturbing months of 1812, had at last rotated back to its right side up."[15]

Understanding and Application

There is a difference between initiative and recklessness. Captain Lawrence's decision to defy his orders and sail for a direct engagement with an equally matched enemy was foolhardy. In all the prior American frigate victories of the war, the captains had been diligent and had used every advantage provided by good seamanship and creative initiative. In some cases, they were even blessed by luck. But by the time Lawrence took over command of the *Chesapeake*, a condition of expectancy had developed. Lawrence gave in to complacency and seemed to operate as though engagement alone was all that was required for victory. His battle readiness was nowhere near that of his enemy, and his lack of respect for both his orders and his adversary was fatal in the end.

The catastrophe of the *Chesapeake* and Lawrence's reckless behavior contains a darker side that emerges when one contemplates the motives for Lawrence's actions. He could not have been primarily interested in strategic advantage for his country or its cause because neither could have been much served by a victory over the *Shannon*. Much glory had already been obtained by American frigate victories over the British, and one more could not add much luster to the already shining reputation of the baby country's navy. In fact, there was much more to lose than to gain by such a conflict. Certainly Lawrence's superiors understood this fact and therefore had given him orders meant to preserve his valuable craft. Why then, the question must be asked, did he do it? Was it for personal glory? Was it motivated by ego and personal gain?

Either Lawrence understood that he could accomplish little more than personal glory from his bravery and acted strictly in his own interest, or else he was blind to the larger strategic situation. Either failing condemns him as a leader — one based on ego, the other on ignorance. The best kind of leader assaults the status quo to pursue a vision of how something ought to be, serving self-interest, of course, but not at the expense of the greater picture. The worst kind of leader does the opposite, serving self-interest despite the greater causes involved, using larger issues and questions as vehicles to propel his or her own personal glory. This is a demonstration of the danger of courage and commitment without convictions. Unless guided by character, the leader's brilliance and abilities will be misapplied.

Leaders exhibit courage but not recklessness. They don't take unnecessary gambles but rather intelligent calculated risks. To do this, it is necessary to remember the big picture or the overall strategic plan. Risking scarce resources for personal glory is not leadership but self-aggrandizement. Courage, pluck, daring, and deftness are much different than gambling, showboating, and strutting. Wise leaders stay in constant touch with this difference.

Summary

There is a spirit of enterprise distinctive of all true leaders, who see what needs to be done and do it without hand-holding or waiting for orders. Action is a keystone of leadership.

The very concept of initiative stands upon the platform of accepting personal responsibility. Leaders function while called upon to make decisions in often confusing situations and possibly dangerous environments, without adequate time and/or information, making decisions to the best of their ability and then striving to make those decisions right. In short, leaders must be able to decide and then take full responsibility for their decisions.

The initiative of a leader also births creativity and ingenuity as the objective remains frozen and the means are molded toward its purpose.

Further, great leaders must have the grander picture in focus, being sure to serve the vision while serving their own interests and keeping the two aligned. This happens automatically when a leader acts according to the convictions of his or her character.

Finally, initiative should never be confused with recklessness, which results from either ego or ignorance.

CHAPTER FOUR

The Lesson of
the Front

Leadership Principle:

Amajor distinction between leadership and management is position. Leaders lead from the front. This is usually true physically but is always true emotionally. The leader is the one who is most committed, who charges out of the foxhole when others delay, who risks danger to accomplish the mission, and who influences others by the magnitude of his or her example and the strength of his or her character. This is necessary for leadership effectiveness because of the power of proximity, which enables accurate information, better communication, group morale, and opportunities for direct-contact influence.

In short, leadership is a hands-on affair.

Illustration #1: King Philip II
and the Spanish Armada

Philip II of Spain had inherited an enormous kingdom from his father, the brilliant Emperor Charles V, in 1556. In 1580, Philip was also crowned king of Portugal. Now he was in charge of not only the largest empire in the world but also its runner-up. It was, to all appearances, an unassailable system of world dominance. But it rested on the thin thread of annual treasure fleets from the New World. Each year, heavy treasure galleons would sail from the New World to Spain loaded with gold and silver from the mines of Mexico and Peru.

Queen Elizabeth I of England, by contrast, ruled a tiny island country that was always short on cash and had little clout or power on the world's stage. She did, however, possess an acute talent for surrounding herself with talent. During her long and prosperous reign, she empowered a rough band of adventurer sailors. These men, including John Hawkins, Walter Raleigh, Martin Frobisher, Charles Howard, Francis Drake, and Richard Grenville, would be largely responsible for the destruction of the old world system and the establishment of the new. It was their prowess upon the seas that struck directly at Spain's vulnerable underbelly and produced such a shift in the balance of power in the world.

Hawkins, along with a young Francis Drake, launched an attack on San Juan de Ulloa, the Mexican coastal spot where the Spanish treasure galleons annually picked up their bullion. This raid, although not entirely successful, had the effect of demonstrating just how vulnerable Spain's treasure galleons were to attack. Elizabeth, always in need of cash and sensing a sly strategic possibility, unleashed her seafarers on the mighty Spanish lifeline in an undeclared sea war.

The attacks began to take an enormous financial toll on Spain, which badly needed the funds for a costly war it was waging in the Netherlands against its hated Protestant enemies. Philip responded to Elizabeth's adventurers by seizing all English ships in Spanish ports and requisitioning them for Spain. Elizabeth then authorized the issuance of "Letters of Marque": official approval for the document's bearer to "set upon by force of arms, and to take and apprehend upon the seas, any of the ships or goods of the subjects of the King of Spain."[1] Over the course of many years, the two monarchs slugged it out in this manner in a seesaw battle of undeclared war followed by overtures of peace followed by further conflict. It was a cycle that would repeat itself many times. Elizabeth, the underdog, wisely bought time and avoided direct confrontation.

This clash of power at sea, however, was only part of the story. There was also a tangled web of family ties and religious conflict that fueled the fight between the two monarchs. The Queen of England prior to Elizabeth had been her half sister Mary, known as "Bloody Mary" for her relentless persecution of her Protestant enemies. Mary also happened to have once been married to Philip II, King of Spain. Upon Mary's death and the ascension of Elizabeth to the English throne, Philip II had lost any influence over England and watched furiously as the country slipped into Protestantism. Further, caught in a plot to assassinate Queen Elizabeth, the Catholic Mary, Queen of Scots (a different Mary), a former Queen of France and Scotland, was executed by Elizabeth's decree. This became Philip's public justification for an open attack on England.

Tired of the quasi-war and feeling it his duty under God to snuff out Protestantism once and for all, Philip decided on an enormous gamble and assumed that God would grant a miracle. Philip launched what he called the Enterprise and what history now calls the Spanish Armada: a massive naval force, the largest the world had ever seen, to transport an army to attack the English mainland directly. It would bear the imprint of both his power and weakness as a leader.

King Philip II was an energetic, dedicated, hard-working taskmaster. In the words of author Stephen Coote:

> ...his unresting capacity for administrative grind was as extraordinary as it was dangerous. At its worst it encouraged his belief that his power might indeed be onmicompetent and could put into effect his unwavering belief that he had been charged by God to uphold the Catholic faith whenever and wherever he could. This duty extended to England.[2]

Philip's leadership style involved cooping himself up in his enormous, monastery-like palace called San Lorenzo de El Escorial and processing the mountainous paperwork of his realm as the central commander of every detail. He had decades of experience as the ruler of the most powerful country in the world, had little ability or patience for personal interaction, and preferred to receive information in writing. He was slow to make decisions, then almost too hasty once he did, and he found it almost impossible to delegate anything. In his time, he was referred to as both the "Bureaucrat King" and "Philip the Prudent" but in our day might more likely be called an obsessive micromanager.

An intricate and complicated affair, the Spanish Armada consisted of amassing an enormous number of ships from multiple ports and then connecting the resultant fleet to a landed army in the Spanish Netherlands under the command of Philip's nephew, the Duke of Parma. The fleet would then protect a flotilla of barges carrying Parma's soldiers across the English Channel until they disembarked for a direct attack. This would all be accompanied by a diversionary raid on Ireland.

Problems with this plan arose almost immediately. Philip's advisors all had differing ideas, and Philip continued to modify and change the invasion plans, blending everyone's ideas until nobody, with the exception of Philip himself, thought the plan likely to succeed. In 1586, Drake's raids on the Spanish Main meant that the treasure ships could not sail at all that year, putting tremendous financial pressure on Philip. Further, there was no system in place through which such a large administrative undertaking as outfitting so many ships and men with munitions and supplies could be accomplished. Everything had to be done manually, from scratch, and almost all of it had to be approved by Philip himself. The mountains of paperwork accompanying the recruitment of 12,000 sailors and 18,000 soldiers; the building of transport barges for an entire army; the amassing of 2,500 artillery pieces, 123,000 rounds of shot, thousands of horses and mules, and thousands of bushels of biscuits, rice, salt pork, and water casks; and the outfitting of 130 ships in multiple ports must have been overwhelming, to say the least. As the slow process of preparation dragged on, it drained Philip's resources along with it, forcing him to borrow money and even sell his late wife's jewels.

With the Armada now being anything but a surprise, Drake led a daring preemptive attack on the Spanish port of Cádiz and destroyed a large amount of shipping and supplies. Drake's success had a major impact on Philip's strategy, forcing him to cancel the diversionary raid on Ireland in favor of having the fleet meet with Parma's army as soon as possible. Everything now hinged upon connecting the fleet of warships, supply ships, and transports with Parma's army of barges and making a successful landing upon English shores.

Next, the Marquis of Santa Cruz, Philip's best admiral, the man who had originally suggested the invasion of England, and Philip's hand-picked leader of the Armada, died of typhus. With the death of Santa Cruz, Philip faced the most potent challenge to the Enterprise yet: a leadership vacuum. Philip chose as Santa Cruz's successor a man that has been interpreted in many different ways by historians. Some have depicted the Duke of Medina Sidonia as incompetent and reluctant, which may be partly true. His military qualifications were minimal, and he had no experience at all with naval warfare. But his actions proved him to be a courageous admiral and an efficient administrator, one willing to contribute massively from his own fortune to the preparations of the fleet.

The main issue, though, seems best articulated by author Arthur Herman:

...Santa Cruz had been a brilliant fleet commander, a man of supreme self-confidence and overreaching ego. If the situation warranted, he did not hesitate to disobey Philip himself. Medina Sidonia lacked that one essential quality of leadership in battle: the willingness to jettison the plan and rely on the killer instinct instead. Medina Sidonia's biggest mistake...was to insist on following Philip's orders to the letter, even when they guaranteed defeat.[3]

Upon assuming command and seeing firsthand the status of the Armada, Medina Sidonia wrote a letter of appeal to Philip, begging him to reconsider launching the attack and sighting a list of thoughtful reasons why he felt it was doomed to failure. He was persuaded, however, not to send it. Philip was determined to proceed, and it was no use bothering him with inconvenient facts. Although the fleet was already, in some cases, running out of water and every ship was short of guns and ammunition, in May of 1588, the largest fleet ever assembled in the age of sail left Spanish ports for the English Channel. Almost no one felt confident of success. Philip himself wrote, "Things hang in the balance....Please God, let the events up there be for His cause, and may He assist us as is so necessary."[4]

A combination of time, space, low rations, a shortage of guns and powder, bad weather, and Elizabeth's adventurer pirates did the rest. The English ships, although inferior in size and tonnage, had superior firepower and longer range guns, allowing them to stand off at a distance and refuse entanglement with the Spanish ships full of dangerous soldiers. The rendezvous with Parma's army never happened, and the ever-dwindling Armada was forced to continue sailing counterclockwise around England and Ireland and limp back home, a mere fraction of what had departed on such hopes of a miracle.

Of the roughly 130 vessels that originally sailed out of Lisbon, at least forty never returned to Spain, and many of the ones that did were beyond repair and left to rot. Most estimates put the total loss of vessels around half the full strength of the original force. The loss of manpower was even more staggering, at two-thirds of the original complement. Estimates suggest that for every Spaniard lost in actual battle, another eight were lost to execution, drowning, disease, starvation, and thirst. Many more died of wounds after making it back to port.

The geopolitical results were also enormous. As author Jacques Mordal so dramatically put it, "Spanish sea-power had suffered a blow from which it never recovered; and as a consequence the vast Spanish Empire...was gradually lost."[5]

Illustration #2: Sir Francis Drake

Francis Drake was almost the exact opposite of King Philip II in every way. Not born not into wealth, nobility, or royalty, Drake would rise high in a world where rising was hardly and rarely done. His lifelong phrase would be, "From small beginnings great things may come."[6]

Drake was brash, bold, and daring, striking where opportunity presented itself — even where and when orders didn't permit. His desire for wealth, fame, and respect would drive him to great achievements but also would garner him great criticism. He was controversial but effective, patriotic but self-serving, dogmatic but egalitarian.

In the long-running conflict between Philip II and Elizabeth, Drake played a major part. His raids on Spanish shipping and coastal towns had brought Philip to fury. To Philip, Drake was a common pirate. To Drake, he himself was the king's rival and chief adversary. Drake's reputation among the Spanish was one of a fearsome corsair, master of the seas and the dread of Spanish ships everywhere, earning him the nickname of "El Draque...the dragon upon the coast."[7] He had also ignited a desire for seafaring adventure across all of England and awakened his countrymen to the importance and possibility of English dominance at sea.

Drake's reputation was based on his results as an efficient and effective fighting commander and an accomplished navigator and seaman. In the words of author Neil Hanson, "...he inspired loyalty and affection among most of his men, and not merely because he made them rich. Even his detractors were forced to admit to his brilliance as a naval commander; if Parma was the greatest land commander of his age, Drake had no peers at sea."[8] Drake pursued unusual efficiency aboard his ships, both in the areas of sailing and gunnery. His practice of drilling his ship's company in the art of firing the ship's great guns brought him criticism for "wasting powder." He was a master of details when he felt the details were important. He planned his operations meticulously, struck quickly and ferociously, hated delays, and understood the overwhelming capabilities of lightning-quick force.

These were the qualities that were instrumental in Drake's effectiveness. However, it was his manner of hands-on command that made these qualities work so well toward his ends. He used the force of his personality and personal power to implement his strategies.

Further, firsthand experience and observation gave Drake the key insight that the ship itself was the potent fighting machine, not the men aboard; the men were simply there to run the machine. Men properly commanded could operate a fighting ship in a way that would be deadly to any enemies. Drake's interpretation of proper command involved sharing the load right alongside his men. In our day and age, it is hard to imagine how revolutionary this concept was in Drake's time. Class distinction, nobility, and the concept that only "commoners" should do work was inherit in the very structure of society. But being on hand, working right alongside his men when necessary, and knowing everything they needed to do better than they knew it themselves, gave Drake credibility with and power over his crews. He was the very embodiment of leadership through influence and ability as much as position. Again, according to Hanson:

> …his own ascent from humble origins also strengthened his revolutionary belief in his oft-stated maxim that a ship's crew must be "of a company," under the command of a single captain, and that the gentlemen and officers must "haul and draw" alongside their seamen. It was inconceivable that any Spanish nobleman would have soiled his hands with such manual work, but initiated by Drake, it had become common practice aboard English ships by the time of the Armada.[9]

Drake's hands-on leadership style, and the loyalty and effectiveness it engendered, spread throughout the English navy. His style was adopted and copied by other captains, and their collective effectiveness became a culture of efficiency and gunnery that would play its part as England's only defense against the enormous Armada.

Understanding and Application

The story of the Spanish Armada could have been different. Its problems were not insurmountable. The Spanish Empire possessed brilliant men and capable commanders, and despite a money crunch resulting largely from the size and scope of the invasion (as well as the ongoing land war in the Spanish Netherlands), Spain still commanded a massive wealth of resources. Philip's leadership, however, was not equal to the task.

It was Philip who generated the inertia that launched the Armada against overwhelming odds. It was Philip's leadership that contributed to the complication, lack of readiness, and lack of morale that produced those odds against success in the first place. Never inspecting the preparations in person and never meeting his commanders and men at their posts, he deprived himself of the knowledge that can only be obtained by firsthand observation. Locked up in his palace processing piles of paperwork, Philip lost the ability to see the facts for what they truly represented, instead of just numbers in ledgers. The result of his centralized, detached, detailed leadership produced a situation in which he automatically deprived himself of the ability to command men through direct influence. He was unable to instill confidence with his presence and to evaluate morale by direct observation.

Finally, without a hands-on analysis, Philip was without the perspective to understand the complications inherent in his plan. He never seems to have grasped the difficulty of connecting a large armada with a land-based army in a tumultuous English Channel filled with hostile English ships. Perhaps if he had seen this directly, his intelligence and usual brilliance could have allotted for these unsurprising but fatal obstacles. Instead, Philip's failure inspired Pope Sixtus to declare that it was "curious that the emperor of half the world should be defied by a woman who was queen of half an island."[10]

Contrast Philip's leadership style to that of Francis Drake's: Where Philip was remote and removed, Drake was present and dangerous. Where Philip's dictatorial, all-knowing self-assumptions left him blind to the complications and weaknesses of his plan, Drake's hands-on command placed him in clear view of his enemy's weaknesses and how to exploit them. Further, Philip's centralized, remote approach to leadership fostered a culture of blind adherence to orders, while Drake's frontal position allowed him to deviate from orders based upon his own observations in a timely and accurate fashion (much as Santa Cruz had been known to do). Finally, Drake's tendency to lead from the front and fight alongside his men created a culture of effectiveness in the English navy that was unmatched by the Spanish.

In the final analysis, then, the failure of the Spanish Armada was a failure of leadership. David Howarth wrote:

This was the intrinsic reason why the armada failed: the king's belief that he could organize a huge operation of war without leaving his study, without consulting anyone, without any human advice, without allowing his commanders to discuss it.... Especially, he did not understand seafaring or navigation—he had never embarked in a ship except as a passenger."[11]

We have seen in earlier chapters that leadership makes a difference, hunger is what drives a leader, and great leaders demonstrate initiative. Philip embodied all of these qualities and beliefs of leadership, but his failure came from his unwillingness to *lead from the front*. Neil Hanson may have said it best:

> Had Philip himself gone to Lisbon to take personal charge of the most complex, important and expensive project of his entire reign, he might have been able to resolve some of the problems that had faced the dying Santa Cruz and his unwilling successor. As it was, despite his insistence on overseeing even the tiniest details of the Enterprise of England, Philip remained in the Escorial [his palace].[12]

Effective leaders know they must lead from the front. Leaders are never afraid to get their hands dirty or to put themselves in harm's way. They know that there are times, especially with stakes high and conditions critical, when the best policy is to take command with their physical presence. There are things that can only be learned by seeing them for one's self. The capability of subordinates and the strength of troop morale might only be properly determined by firsthand contact. Belief, inspiration, courage, and action can often only be conjured among followers by an actual demonstration or showing of the leader's commitment. If example is a chief lever in influencing others, it must, at least occasionally, be demonstrated physically and in person. Ignorance of this fact, or cowardice in the face of it, can be fatal to a leader's vision. Hard work, dedication, and administrative attentiveness will not take the place of a leader's responsibility to actually lead.

Leading from the front also engenders a culture of leadership credibility that leads to great efficiencies and timeliness of course corrections. Leaders on hand can see opportunities and chances for advancement that otherwise would be missed and lost. Over time and across a large organization, these gains can accumulate into enormous advantages.

Illustration #3: Lord Admiral Nelson and His Fleet Battles

No other commander in the age of fighting sail embodies the concept and commitment of leading from the front quite like Horatio Nelson, who became a legend in the English Royal Navy more than two centuries after the Spanish Armada. The first English commander to radically depart from the time-tested *Fighting Instructions*, Nelson pioneered an extremely aggressive approach to naval warfare. His philosophy swung on a distinction: the difference between fighting and annihilation.

The *Fighting Instructions* had taught that the most effective sea battle involved aligning one's fleet in single file while sailing alongside a similarly arranged enemy fleet and firing at each ship in turn. This inflicted damage to an enemy fleet while limiting losses to one's own. Nelson's approach, however, was much more daring. He favored

123

breaking his fleet into two single-file lines and then sailing them in parallel and directly at the enemy's ships. The opponent, expecting the age-old "line of battle" as practiced for decades, would comply by aligning its own fleet in a single long line. Nelson's two lines would then pierce the enemy line at an angle in two locations, slicing the line into three discordant groups. Because of the wind and the effort required to "beat back against the wind," the front third of the enemy ships would be out of contention for a while and unable to return to the aid of their fellow ships being attacked to their rear. As each of Nelson's ships going through the enemy line would sail past the front and rear of opposing ships, it would pour in its "broadsides" of firepower (firing all the cannon from that side of the ship). This tactic, known as "raking," was the deadliest in naval warfare.

Of all the descriptions of the terrifying battles of that age, none are as gruesome and horrific as those of a ship being raked by enemy fire. The front and rear of wooden fighting ships were notoriously vulnerable. They were armed with small "chaser" guns that were meant for long-range harassment instead of close-range firepower and defense, and there was very little protective planking of any kind, especially at the stern. As a result, there wasn't much a ship's company could do under raking fire except duck for cover. Only there was little or no cover to be had. A ship made of wood, even solid oak timbers and planking, was little protection against heavy, hot, fast-moving cannonballs, barrel shot, chain shot, and shrapnel. Often, wooden splinters caused by the impact of these projectiles were the most dangerous of all. As the guns of an enemy ship would fire in succession down the unprotected length of a ship, munitions and scattering splinters could kill or wound every man aboard the upper decks.

After passing through the enemy line and inflicting massive damage by raking fire, Nelson's captains were then to sail up the opposite side of the enemy's line while other ships sailed along the closer side. In this way, Nelson's fleet would double-up on enemy vessels. The final piece of the "Nelson Touch" was his instruction that if things got confusing and pell-mell, captains were to lie as close as possible to an enemy and destroy it with superior gunnery.

Nelson's tactics were horribly effective, but they also required a special kind of mettle from his commanders. This was because as his attacking ships approached the enemy line, there was a distinct period of time when they were in range of enemy guns but unable to return fire. This danger was compounded by the tradition in the age of fighting sail, and perpetuated fanatically by Nelson's own example, of the captain and his staff standing out on the open quarterdeck throughout the entirety of a battle action. The quarterdeck was an open-air platform at the stern of the ship and the second highest deck on a ship of the line. From this position, the captain and his command staff could survey the battle around them and be in close contact with the coxswain, who was responsible for relaying the captain's orders to the various crews aboard ship.

For the purpose of communication and command, it was an ideal spot. From the standpoint of danger and risk, it could hardly have been worse. Not only was the quarter-deck entirely exposed to the large guns of the enemy, but it was also a literal shooting gallery for riflemen perched high in the "tops" of enemy ships. Adam Nicolson wrote:

> These places were where the killing and wounding was done and so among these ranks, in ship after ship, the proportion of casualties often rose to well over a third or even half. The more significant the man...the more vulnerable he was. It is precisely the opposite of generals commanding later battles from many tens of miles behind the front. Here the commanders placed themselves on the point of the spear.[13]

With Nelson's tactics, the situation was even worse. His penchant for splitting enemy lines of battle and getting into position to rake enemy ships, followed by close-action gunnery, placed him and his commanders as much in harm's way as could be imagined.

The reputation of the prowess of the Royal Navy and the smashing successes of Nelson destroying entire enemy fleets produced awe in his opponents. This intimidation factor was further enhanced by the bravery shown by Nelson as he insisted on his ship being the first to break the enemy line and take the brunt of the fresh, fully-prepared and waiting enemy fire, and nearly every one of his captains demonstrated the same eagerness to lead from the front.

Understanding and Application

History holds few examples of leading from the front as striking as Nelson during his epic fleet battles. In particular, the Battle of Trafalgar was his culminating masterpiece. Although fatal to Nelson, it was instrumental in his immortality in the pages of history. While fully exposed on the quarterdeck of his flagship the *Victory*, the first to break the enemy line, he was killed by a musket ball fired from the top of an enemy ship. In this action, Nelson had almost literally been the point of the spear.

The danger of leading from the front may be severe but will always be inspiring and speak more about the leader's commitment than any mere words. Most important, though, are the results. Nelson's bravery and aggressive fighting methods produced confidence in his fellow and subordinate commanders.

This is the result of leading from the front. In a massive battle such as Trafalgar, with literally scores of ships and thousands of men involved, Nelson and his captains couldn't have done it all. There were nearly 17,000 Englishmen involved in the battle. A leader's job is to influence others toward a goal. Nelson's example, his influence on his captains, and their subsequent example trickled down through the ranks and resulted in a culture of courage and action. Roy Adkins wrote, "Nelson might have provided the inspiration and example, but it was the thousands of ordinary men and women aboard the ships who made the difference."[14] That is the legacy of leading from the front.

Illustration #4: Sir Hyde Parker and Lord Nelson at the Battle of Copenhagen

In chapter two, we discussed the Battle of Copenhagen. It was Nelson's last victory before his death at the pinnacle Battle of Trafalgar four years later and was his closest brush with real defeat. What became an English victory was very close to being a disaster.

Much of humanity's struggle against itself, and of warfare in particular, is marked by intense effort on both sides, with each side near defeat, wondering how much longer it can hold out against an opponent that appears tougher and more resilient. The facts, usually, can be quite different than they appear. Each side is typically nearer the point of collapse than its enemies think. At such a critical moment, it is usually leadership and willpower that make the difference. Massive battles have turned on a 1 percent difference in ability, initiative, or determination properly timed. Success is sometimes just a matter of hanging on a second longer than the competition.

The Battle of Copenhagen was one such battle. The English naval forces greatly underestimated the fighting strength and determination of the Danes. The shore batteries, reserve gunmen, and fighting spirit of the Danish defenders had the attacking English ships on the doorway of defeat. For once, Nelson's initiative and daring appeared to have gotten him in over his head.

As you'll recall, Sir Hyde Parker, the senior commander of the English fleet, stood off at a distance aboard his flagship. Parker and a complement of his deeper draught ships had remained in reserve and in defense of a possible attack from any Russian fleets from the north. These bigger ships would also have been unable to make the southerly attack that Nelson had conceived and in fact led with smaller craft. With these valid reasons for standing off, Parker was still in a position that put him at a disadvantage for leadership. Nelson was his next in command and, by leading the attacking squadron, had become the commander of the assault. While Parker was the senior officer by position, Nelson was in command by proximity.

It was at the peak of the battle, when both sides were pouring in their firepower with full effort, casualties were mounting alarmingly, confusion was at its highest, and fatigue settled in heavily, that the battle turned. Although the Danes's fire was steady, they were about to give in. At that same point, however, there were three English ships that had run aground and several others flying signals of distress. It was the critical moment for the English to hang in there and see it through to the end. Besides, they had maneuvered themselves into a position that would allow no safe retreat. Under the shore guns of the Danish, any English ship trying to make sail and extract itself would have been blown to pieces.

Sir Parker, looking on from a distance at more than three hours of intense fighting, began to panic. From his perspective, the fleet was in trouble and taking the worst of it. Sensing defeat, he gave his famous signal to break off the engagement. Nelson, in the middle of the mêlée, had a more accurate picture. He knew that his fleet was giving at least as much as it was getting. Even though some of his ships were aground and others were badly mangled, most of them were still able to engage the enemy with deadly fire. As a result, he famously ignored the signal to disengage. This disobedience of orders put him at grave personal risk with his superiors, and he knew it. However, Nelson understood that the danger to his fleet was even greater and more immediate.

Being at the front and engaged personally, Nelson had the advantage of perspective. It was the critical point in the battle. And in less than an hour, the battle was over.

Understanding and Application

There is a timeliness to success. Great victories often come from small differences. Great leaders find ways to hang on longer than their competition, getting every ounce of ability out of their organizations toward the goal. Even when things seem perilous, leaders can press forward just a little further or a little while longer as if they can be sure they are not yet defeated. This important judgment of ability can only be made by acquiring the type of information that comes from firsthand observation and discernment. This takes leading from the front.

Leaders who lead from the front have the advantage of perspective and clarity in situations that would otherwise appear cloudy. In complicated situations against determined adversaries or with significant challenges, great leaders know they must gain every advantage. Being on hand and present themselves provides an invaluable window into the reality they face. The closer a leader's map is to the actual territory, the better his or her information upon which to make decisions. The quality of those decisions is paramount to success. The leader who has the courage to lead from the front will always have the advantage on the leader who plays it safe from the rear.

Summary

The best leaders know they must, at least at times, lead from the front. This gives the advantage of credibility among the ranks. When people see leaders willing to do what they do and run the risks they run, it builds morale. When leaders are on hand to demonstrate their own competency, it enhances their authority from being positional to being earned.

Further, leaders who lead from the front gain information and perspective that is available no other way. Sometimes, a leader just has to see for him- or herself. This is especially important when timing is critical, when major decisions have to be made quickly, when the project is enormous, when the decisions are of the highest importance, when defeat or victory are equally as close, and when no one else is available to make sense of the situation at hand.

Communication, too, is the clearest for the leader who is on the scene. Seeing the facts as they really are, a leader

131

can quickly disseminate his or her decisions to the ranks with the least amount of ambiguity or delay. Further, there is almost no way to measure the importance of leadership by proximity, when a leader's personal touch can influence others directly. This builds morale, confidence, and belief in the leader and his or her vision. At many points in a leader's career, he or she will have to be wise enough to know when to lead by being there in person, by being at the front.

Finally, leaders who lead from the front get copied and duplicated by other leaders. This multiplies the effectiveness of the organization overall and creates a culture of leadership effectiveness.

CHAPTER FIVE

The Lesson of Discernment

Leadership Principle:

Leaders must cultivate the ability to make good decisions. This requires the ability to discern between multiple options that may all appear to have near-equal merit. It will also occasionally require going against accepted procedures or violating orders.

Rules are a double-edged sword; great leaders understand both edges and make their decisions accordingly. Discernment comes with experience and a clear understanding of principles and objectives. Leaders who comprehend the bigger picture and their role in it develop the ability to discern between the challenging choices with which they are confronted.

Illustration #1: The Line Ahead Battle Formation

The history of warfare at sea went through several phases. In the age of fighting sail, tactics went from battles at sea mimicking those on land to a whole new way of fighting that adapted to the particulars of sailing vessels and their technology. A fighting style that harmonized the complications of the wind, weather, waves, and the sheer complexity of the sailing battle ship was needed. The style that resulted could best be called a tactic, and it evolved over decades of experience derived from actual warfare.

Somewhere between the first and second Dutch Wars in the middle of the seventeenth century, the line ahead formation was developed and adopted, first by the English Royal Navy and then by its enemies. This formation complicated command and communication but enhanced a fleet's fighting effectiveness. As Michael A. Palmer wrote:

> ...naval officers faced imposing tactical dilemmas. They had to operate, in combat, the sailing man-of-war—the most sophisticated machine yet developed. They had to do so in an environment in which a mistake or ill fortune could lead to the destruction of the fleet by the elements. And they had to operate on a global scale."[1]

These were indeed perilous challenges, probably more so than those faced by commanders of armies on the land, and therefore required specific solutions particular to the strengths and weaknesses of sailing battle ships.

The line ahead formation evolved to comprehend these challenges. It also took advantage of the inherent fighting style of a man-of-war. The ship's guns were arranged along its axis on its decks and pointed outward from its sides. Thus a man-of-war was restricted to attacking its enemies by turning broadside. It is from this orientation that the term "giving them a broadside" was derived. A wooden fighting ship would sail near an enemy ship, turn its side to the enemy, and fire the guns along that side. The line ahead formation took this particular into account and applied it to an entire fleet. The resulting tactic was to line up all the ships in a fleet in a single file and then sail that line alongside the enemy fleet. As each ship passed an enemy ship, it would "deliver a broadside" and sail forward to attack the next prey in the enemy's line.

Figure 4: The French Line (Left) and British Line (Right)
Engaged in the Battle of Chesapeake Bay, 1781

The first real battle that employed this arrangement was a battle off Gabbard Shoal in which the English achieved victory by destroying or capturing twenty enemy ships. Even more significant, the English ships survived the battle in such good condition that they were able to stay at sea afterward—a feat almost unheard of in previous naval engagements, whether victor or vanquished. From then on, the "line" increasingly became the standard mode of operation. The official *Fighting Instructions* of the Royal Navy canonized the line ahead formation for generations to come.

Parallel to the development of the line ahead formation and largely responsible for the Royal Navy's continued reliance upon it was a shift in naval leadership capabilities. From the time of Queen Elizabeth in the sixteenth century through the Dutch Wars in the seventeenth, the British Royal Navy became less a band of adventurers with authority based on their own accomplishments and more a bureaucracy filled with commanders of noble birth. This meant that those in command had not earned their positions by achievement. Leadership became more a matter of who one was rather than what one had accomplished. With this decrease in ability and the shrinking of the meritocracy that had given the Royal Navy its initiative and pluck, procedures and rules were necessary. The *Fighting Instructions* and the line ahead formation were there to provide the experience lacking in the commanders.

As with all procedures, however, the line ahead had some drawbacks. It allowed incompetent or hesitant commanders to avoid battle if conditions didn't present themselves perfectly for a line ahead engagement. It could also stifle the initiative of individual commanders by disallowing their creativity and variations of the procedure.

One example historians routinely use to illustrate the suppressing effect of the line ahead is Admiral Graves at the Battle of the Chesapeake in the American Revolution. We already covered this battle in depth in chapter one and won't rehash it here. The point to remember is that English Admiral Graves found himself in position to attack the French fleet led by de Grasse. Graves had the advantage of the "weather gauge," (the wind at his back allowing superior maneuverability) and the last best chance to save the stranded army of Cornwallis. The situation didn't present itself quite as succinctly as the line ahead required, and the signaling system used by the English caused confusion in Graves's ranks. The result was a light skirmish with little result and the abandonment of Cornwallis to his defeat at the hands of the French and Americans. Historian John A. Tilley wrote, "Perhaps Graves' mind…was so infested with the sanctified doctrine of the line of battle and the *Fighting Instructions* that he was incapable of imagining how to fight in any other manner." Michael Lewis added, "In the whole history of sailing-warfare no rigid adherence to the line was ever more fatal than that of…Graves."[2]

In Graves's defense, there were other factors besides. But the common practice procedures had proven to be a rigid template that wouldn't work in all situations. Procedures took the place where a leader's creativity and ingenuity were needed.

All in all, however, the line ahead worked successfully. With slight modifications, based upon the commander, the line ahead formation remained the standard for years without significant challenge to its fundamental assumptions. Some, such as Admiral Edward Hawke at Quiberon Bay, allowed their captains to depart from the strict guidelines of the line ahead and encouraged and relied upon their individual initiative. Hawke was able to do this partly because his captains and crews were so finely tuned from their many months at sea maintaining his blockade of Brest, as discussed earlier. He also properly surmised that his ships could safely follow the enemy ships that were retreating into port because they would know the safest route to follow. Further, although it was getting dark and a storm was beginning, Hawke realized that the initiative and battle readiness of his captains would suffice. Hawke's daring and smashing success at Quiberon Bay, resulting from his willingness to improvise on the age-old line ahead formation to suit conditions, was a clear picture of the discernment of a leader.

There would be another who would demonstrate an even more radical departure from the tried-and-tested old procedure: Horatio Nelson. It is impossible that a leader like Nelson not show up in many of the illustrations of leadership principles in a book such as this. His departure from the line ahead formation and his daring preference for a "pell-mell" battle were the very foundation of his fame.

We've already discussed in chapter three his exploits at the Battle of Cape St. Vincent, where he broke from protocol to board not just one but two ships. In chapter four, we briefly mentioned his unorthodox style, which you'll read more about in later chapters as we highlight his most famous battles, the Battle of the Nile and the Battle of Trafalgar. Nelson knew the *Fighting Instructions* as well, if not better, than any naval commander of his time. But he used them as a reference rather than slavishly adhering to them. He used his discernment during the thick of battle to make snap decisions and alter his tactics. Had he adhered to the line ahead formation in his famous battles, they would have undoubtedly resulted in drastically different outcomes.

Understanding and Application

The line ahead formation was developed to maximize fighting effectiveness and minimize damage to a fleet. It was a successful tactic developed over a long period of time in actual battle conditions, and it was necessary to compensate for a lack of creative and committed commanders. Its strengths also produced its weaknesses, as with most procedures and regulations. Some commanders, such as Graves, were stifled by it and deprived of important battle victories. Others, such as Hawke and Nelson, modified and completely replaced common practice to come up with their own successful formulas. This required daring, innovation, and most of all, discernment.

Leaders understand that rules and regulations have a purpose. In many conditions, following them is the wisest course of action. After all, utilizing the experience of others is often a shortcut to success and the model of prudence. But what happens when procedures don't quite fit the situation? What does a leader do then? Many leaders stick to the book, play it safe, and miss out on opportunity. The great leaders, however, possess a keen sense of when rules are to be followed and when they are to be broken. There are certainly two edges to procedures and regulations: one that cuts when they are not followed and one that cuts when they are. Discernment is knowing which edge to respect and when. Only the great leaders have the courage and the wisdom to know the difference and to take advantage of it at the right time.

How did Hawke realize it was time to shift away from the rigid restrictions of the line ahead formation? How did Nelson know it would work to bring on a total engagement and depart entirely from the procedures in the *Fighting Instructions*? Real leaders, either through experience, bravery, vision, or some combination of them all, seem to possess the ability to know just when to follow proven paths and when to depart from them. They understand that timing of an action can be as important as the action itself. They develop a feel for what is needed and when, remaining always ready to innovate and create when necessary. Bravery is necessary to depart from procedures, and a quality of persistence is often needed to see the decision through.

Discernment is very difficult to teach and can only be learned by degrees. It is hard to describe but easily spotted. Discernment, therefore, falls into the "art" side of leadership. It requires an overall vision and a high picture of the theatre of action. It requires an understanding of priorities and the ability to sift through the question of what to leave in and what to leave out. It requires creativity, initiative, boldness, and persistence. And it requires good judgment, clear thinking, and the acceptance of the responsibility for outcomes.

Illustration #2: The Failure to Conquer Sailors' Worst Enemy

To sailors in the age of fighting sail, there was an enemy to be feared more than rival combatants, cannon fire, musket balls, grapeshot, and cutlasses combined. Between 1500 and 1800, this enemy is estimated to have killed at least two million sailors. During the eighteenth century, this enemy killed more British sailors than enemy action. In George Anson's voyage of 1740–1742, this enemy killed more than two-thirds of his crew (1,300 out of 2,000) within the first ten months of the voyage. During the Seven Years' War (1754–1763), the Royal Navy enlisted 184,999 sailors, of which 133,708 were killed by this enemy.

If you were responsible for the lives of sailors during this time, you would think that conquering this enemy would be your number-one priority. But strangely, naval leaders put far more focus on tactics and strategies for capturing enemy ships and sailors than on this killer.

The enemy I'm referring to is scurvy. A disease resulting from a deficiency of vitamin C, which causes malaise, lethargy, skin spots, spongy gums and loss of teeth, bleeding from the mucous membranes, neuropathy, and, most important, death, scurvy has a fascinating history. Over the centuries, cures for scurvy have been repeatedly discovered and then forgotten.

The disease was first documented by Hippocrates as early as the fifth century BC. Crusaders in the thirteenth century suffered frequently from scurvy. In Vasco da Gama's 1497 expedition, sailors understood that citrus fruit had a curative effect on the disease. In 1536, while exploring the St. Lawrence River in Canada, the French explorer Jacques Cartier and his men were saved from the disease by local natives, who taught them to make a tea from the needles of White Cedar trees, which are high in vitamin C. In 1593, Admiral Sir Richard Hawkins taught his men to drink orange and lemon juice to prevent scurvy.

Without being able to isolate vitamin C, doctors and scientists did not understand why these acidic substances cured scurvy but only that they were effective. In 1614, John Woodall, Surgeon General of the East India Company, published a handbook for apprentice surgeons aboard company ships in which he recommended fresh food when available and when not, oranges, lemons, limes, and tamarinds—and, as a last resort, sulfuric acid. (The belief was that the acid, not vitamin C, had the curative effect, and therefore any acid would do.) Physician Johann Bachstrom published a book on scurvy in 1734, stating that "scurvy is solely owing to a total abstinence from fresh vegetable food, and greens, which is alone the primary cause of the disease"[3] and urging the use of fresh fruits and vegetables as a cure.

In the 1740s, James Lind began clinical trials—the first controlled experiments in the history of medicine—to discover the cause and a cure for the disease. By 1747, he had proven that scurvy could be treated and prevented with citrus fruit. He officially published his findings in 1753 and then attempted to sell lime juice as a medicine. But because the vitamin C in his juice became oxidized, it had no effect in treating scurvy, and therefore the Royal Navy did not adopt the solution until the 1790s. The belief that any acid would have a curative effect on scurvy persisted in Britain into the late nineteenth century.

The first major long-distance voyage without a fatal outbreak of scurvy was made by Spanish naval officer Alessandro Malaspina, whose medical officer, Pedro González, was convinced that fresh oranges and lemons prevented the disease. It wasn't until the Napoleonic Wars (1803-1815) that scurvy was finally eradicated from the Royal Navy, due to the efforts of Gilbert Blane, the chairman of the Royal Navy's Sick and Hurt Board, who implemented the use of fresh lemons. Interestingly, the remarkable health improvement that ensued among sailors played a critical role in subsequent naval battles, notably the Battle of Trafalgar. In 1867, the British passed the Merchant Shipping Act, which required all ships of the Royal Navy and Merchant Navy to provide a daily lime ration to sailors to prevent scurvy. The term "limey," referring to British sailors, derives from this practice.

But even after the 1867 act, British sailors continued to suffer from scurvy well into the twentieth century. The reasons were because the belief still prevailed that the acid did the trick, and much of the lime juice used aboard ships was exposed to light and air, thus oxidizing and reducing the vitamin C content. In fact, in 1918, an experiment was performed using samples of the Navy and Merchant Marine's lime juice and showed that it had virtually no antiscorbutic power. It wasn't until the belief that scurvy was a nutritional deficiency, best treated by eating fresh food, particularly fresh citrus or fresh meat, became universal in the early twentieth century that scurvy began disappearing for good. The reason why was not discovered until ascorbic acid (vitamin C) was isolated in 1932 by Hungarian biochemist Szent-Györgyi and found to be the antiscorbutic agent (rather than mere acid).

Understanding and Application

This may seem like somewhat of an odd example to use for the principle of discernment. But when you think about it, it's actually quite a profound and useful example. When more sailors are dying from scurvy than combat, wouldn't you think that you should pour resources into finding a cure for the disease?

One primary job of a leader is to discern where resources are needed the most to have the greatest impact on the objectives. This example is akin to a software company today pouring all its resources into creating superior technology when its people are leaving in droves because of a diseased culture. In this case, superior technology depends on a superior team; until the leader cures the culture, the technology cannot be created.

Perhaps one reason why Britain's Royal Navy, or any singular country, for that matter, did not allocate resources toward finding a cure for scurvy is that the navies of *all* nations suffered from the same disease. In other words, if a problem is the same for you and all your competitors — if none of your competitors have an advantage when it comes to this problem — why seek a solution?

But this is where the discernment of a leader is critical. The fact that British sailors were healthier and suffered less from scurvy than their combatants played a critical role in the Battle of Trafalgar. When leaders can find areas for improvement that their competitors ignore, superiority can be achieved. Sometimes, the place to focus is not where leaders traditionally focus (e.g. superior technology, greater capital, improved production processes, etc.) but rather on overlooked areas that can have a dramatic impact on productivity and results. This requires discernment on the part of the leader to analyze his or her organization and determine critical areas that must be addressed.

Illustration #3: Thomas Cochrane and the Capture of the *Gamo*

Englishman Thomas Cochrane's first command was the tiny brig misnamed the *Speedy*. It was actually quite slow and difficult to handle. But this fact hadn't stopped Cochrane and his crew from amassing an impressive string of victories, capturing scores of enemy vessels along

Spain's Mediterranean coast. In fact, their successes had been so numerous that the crew of the *Speedy* was at about half strength, the remainder of the men having been sent off as "prize crews" responsible for sailing the captured crafts back to home ports. There were barely enough men left on board to sail the ship. The *Speedy* and its plucky commander had become more than a nuisance to the Spanish, whose trade had been significantly interrupted by the capture of nearly fifty ships in less than a year.

On the one-year anniversary of his command, Cochrane was in pursuit of two Spanish gunboats that fled into the harbor of Barcelona. Apparently acting as decoys, the gunboats led the *Speedy* into the path of a thirty-two-gun Spanish frigate named *El Gamo*, which had been sent out in search of Cochrane. The *Gamo* was four times the size of the *Speedy* and had more than 300 sailors and marines on board, compared to Cochrane's mere forty-eight. Whereas the *Speedy* had only fourteen guns, *El Gamo* had thirty-two. The capability of the guns was all out of proportion as well, with the broadside of the *Gamo* being 190 pounds to the *Speedy's* twenty-eight. (A broadside was the total weight of shot capable of being fired from one side of a ship's guns and was a common measure of firepower.)

Being too close to the larger ship to run for safety, Cochrane surprised his crew by deciding to turn and fight rather than surrender. According to biographer Donald Thomas, "The one factor in Cochrane's favour was the improbability of what he was about to do. The officers of the *Gamo* would never believe that anyone but a lunatic would try to attack them with a brig whose mastheads hardly reached much above their own quarterdeck."[4] Cochrane sailed in close to windward (the side offering the advantage of the wind), and to cause confusion, he flew the American flag. Flying the colors of other countries, particularly a neutral one like the United States, was a common ruse during the age of fighting sail. Nonetheless, it caused hesitation on the part of the *Gamo*. For the moment, the menacing gun ports of the Spanish ship remained silent. Then Cochrane turned the *Speedy* and came around on the leeward side of the Spanish, giving the *Gamo* the wind advantage — another move designed to confuse. At this point, Cochrane quickly had his crew raise the British flag.

As the *Speedy* sailed closer at high speed, it somehow survived the first broadside of the larger ship. This was by design. Cochrane had surrendered the coveted "weather gauge" by giving the Spanish ship the windward position, and he purposely took the leeward side. Although battle maneuvers were more difficult from that side, it was also harder for a ship in the *Gamo's* position to fire at an enemy so close to leeward. The wind heeled the ship over, and shots were likely to go into the sea.

Cochrane told his men to hold their fire, and he instructed them to double-shot their guns. This meant they would have less of a firing range but would spew forth twice the amount of projectiles and have the potential for causing much more destruction. "Grape" or "grapeshot" was a mixture of metal pieces and balls designed to scatter like a shotgun blast and inflict maximum damage to personnel and rigging. A double-shot dose of it, properly aimed, would be deadly to all in its path. It was risky to sail in close enough to use a double-shot broadside, but it just might give the *Speedy* a chance.

A second broadside from the *Gamo* had no effect on the charging *Speedy*, which was approaching as though it meant to ram the bigger vessel. Then there was a crash as the masts and rigging of the two ships entangled upon impact. The *Gamo's* guns fired again, but the shot went over the heads of all aboard the tiny *Speedy* and only damaged sails and rigging. Finally, the *Speedy* aimed its comparatively little four-pounders as high as possible and fired. Because of the angle of the shots, upward and through the *Gamo's* gun ports, the effect was devastating. The flooring under some of the Spanish guns was blown upward as the grapeshot scattered in its deadly patterns. The captain of the *Gamo* was killed instantly. The firing continued furiously from both sides, but because of the mismatch in size and gun position, the *Speedy* inflicted more damage.

Because of the ineffectiveness of their firing, soldiers aboard the *Gamo* made three attempts to board the *Speedy* and force a hand-to-hand fight. Each time, however, Cochrane would let the Spanish assemble for the jump across and then maneuver his ship to widen the gap of ocean between. Once perched in such a position, musket and small arms fire from the *Speedy* would wipe out the would-be attackers.

The fight continued in this manner for over an hour. Then, according to Cochrane, "The great disparity of force rendering it necessary to adopt some measure that might prove decisive, I resolved to board."[5] His men, in disbelief over what they had so far achieved, enthusiastically responded to this practically suicidal order.

Cochrane split his men into two groups, leaving only the ship's surgeon aboard and at the wheel. One group, with faces painted black for effect, went to the front and climbed aboard the *Gamo* from the bow. The other, led by Cochrane himself, climbed straight up the side of the Spanish ship. In the smoke, noise, and confusion, the Spanish were unnerved by the screaming black faces rushing at them from the front of their ship while they were engaged with attackers from the side as well.

In the tight quarters aboard the deck of the *Gamo*, the superior numbers of the Spanish could not be brought to full advantage. Even so, Cochrane was not out of surprises. In the middle of the mêlée, he called over to the only man left aboard the *Speedy* and instructed him, very loudly, to send the second wave of attackers. Somehow the recipient of the bogus order managed to contain his surprise and pretended to comply with loud shouts and orders to sailors who didn't exist. Many of the Spanish apparently concluded that the *Speedy* had been packed with marines and the whole battle had been a trap.

Next, someone noticed that the Spanish ensign was being lowered from the mast: the sign of surrender. But it wasn't the Spanish who were lowering it. Rather, it was one of Cochrane's men who had previously been instructed to do so at a proper point in the struggle. Before they could figure out that it was a trick, the disheartened Spanish, with their captain dead, laid down their weapons. Afraid the Spanish would discover how few had defeated them, Cochrane and his men were quick to shuttle the Spanish below decks, where they were held in position with the *Gamo's* two largest guns.

The tiny little *Speedy* proceeded to the British port in Minorca, towing a prize ship four times its size. Donald Thomas wrote:

> The *Gamo* should have been able to blow the *Speedy* out of the water before the British ship came near enough to fire a shot. The Spanish troops should have been able to overwhelm the depleted crew of the brig as soon as she came alongside. A man who was so foolish as to lead forty-eight seamen on board an enemy ship with a crew of more than 300 ought to have found himself and his men prisoners within a few minutes."[6]

But it didn't happen that way. Instead, Cochrane had pulled off what Nathan Miller called "the finest single-ship action of the Napoleonic Wars."[7]

Figure 5: The *Speedy* Capturing the *Gamo* 1801 by Charles Dixon

Understanding and Application

Certainly, Cochrane's bold and surprising attack of the *Gamo* displays courage, initiative, and creativity—almost to the point of recklessness. But when you understand the context, you see how it was not reckless at all but rather wise and discerning. Cochrane's attack wasn't the action of a suicidal kamikaze; he actually believed he could win, and he knew exactly how. He recognized how his smaller size could actually be turned into great advantage. He immediately discerned that, by giving the *Gamo* the wind advantage, he could sail his much smaller vessel underneath its cannon fire. He realized that every shot would have to count and thus had his sailors double-pack their guns and wait until the last possible moment to fire. He used trickery to confound the Spanish and maintain the advantage throughout the battle.

The actions of leaders often carry great consequences. Had Cochrane lost the battle with the *Gamo*, he would have been condemned as a lunatic, vilified for leading men to their deaths in such a reckless and irresponsible manner. But he immediately sized up the situation and, through his power of discernment, realized how and where he could ply advantage.

A leader's job is to achieve the objectives. But doing so in a reckless manner actually jeopardizes the objectives. In the heat of battle, a leader must stay calm and cool. He must not be discouraged by competition or distracted by irrelevant data. He must size up a situation and discern where and how he can have the greatest impact. He must determine how seeming disadvantages can be turned into advantages. In short, a leader must have more than fiery courage; he must also have cool-headed wisdom.

Summary

One of the most critical skills leaders must develop is the ability to make the right decisions — especially under fire. They must learn to see not just two or a handful of options but a multiplicity of them. They must be able to weigh the merits of each. Then, they must know which option to choose.

In many cases, this may require going against protocol, breaking rules, violating orders. Hence, a leader must also be aware of the consequences of his decisions and actions.

It is precisely this awareness that allows a leader to break rules when a situation demands it; a good leader would rather face criticism from superiors than lose people and battles because he failed to make the right decision in the heat of battle.

Leaders are not rigid dogmatists but rather flexible pragmatists. They hold their integrity, principles, values, and ideals inviolate. But when it comes to strategies, tactics, and procedures, they do what it takes to achieve the objectives—even if it means breaking the rules. They do this because they understand the *why* behind rules. They see the big picture. They don't necessarily flaunt rules, but neither do they worship them.

Great leaders make decisions that, in the moment, appear to others to be foolhardy and reckless. But when the smoke clears, their decisions are actually realized to be less a product of courage than a product of wisdom and discernment.

CHAPTER SIX

The Lesson of Concentration

Leadership Principle:

To be ineffective, leaders don't have to make poor decisions—choosing the wrong thing to do at the wrong time. Often, what renders leaders ineffective is simply dividing their energy and focus—trying to do too many good things at once, while failing to identify the best and most important thing to do at any given moment.

A vital skill of leadership is the ability to comb through mounds of data, sift through complexity, analyze all possible options, and then prioritize them. And once they have created priorities, leaders must focus their energy and attention on the most important one. Leaders can be skilled tacticians, but if their overarching strategy is not clear, coherent, and focused, their tactics will fail.

Leaders have an obsessive focus on one clear and supreme objective. They bring all their resources to bear on the fulfillment of that objective. They concentrate all their forces on the strategic battles that can win the war.

Illustration #1: Concentration of Forces at the Battle of the Bay

In chapter one, we explored how a French naval commander, Vice-Admiral François-Joseph-Paul, comte de Grasse, was largely responsible for winning the final battle of the Revolutionary War by sailing, on his own initiative, from his post in the Caribbean to Chesapeake Bay. There, he was able to assist George Washington's troops in trapping General Cornwallis at Yorktown, Virginia.

In addition to the leadership lessons we've already extracted from this story, there is yet another lesson to be learned.

Admiral Thomas Graves, the commander of the British fleet during that final and fateful battle, has received much criticism from historians for his strict adherence to the line ahead formation, which utterly failed under the conditions. But in truth, Graves's tactical errors were not the deciding factor of that battle. The outcome of that battle was ultimately determined by the superior *strategy* of the combined American and French forces, not a failure of *tactics* on the part of the British. As Michael A. Palmer wrote, "The merits of French policy and strategy were equaled only by the shortcomings of those of the British."[1] In short, Graves was set up to fail by one fact: the French had concentrated virtually all of their naval forces where it mattered most, while the British failed to comprehend the importance of that critical battleground and thus failed to bring sufficient resources to bear.

Admiral Rodney, the British commander in the Caribbean, had spotted de Grasse's fleet leaving the Caribbean en route to America but failed to engage his ships, assuming that de Grasse would divide his fleet and send only a portion to the Americans. Rodney correctly guessed that the French were headed to Chesapeake Bay to assist Washington, but his warning to Graves was intercepted. He ordered another English commander in the Caribbean to dispatch five ships and five frigates to the bay, but that order was disobeyed. Admiral Hood had been sent to head off de Grasse in the bay, but he beat him there and continued sailing to New York. Even when the English discovered that the French were concentrating their fleet in the Chesapeake, they delayed in getting there. General Cornwallis missed an opportunity to escape Yorktown before the siege set in.

In contrast, the Americans and the French understood the importance of Yorktown. De Grasse defied all common wisdom and made a number of unpredictable moves in order to move his fleet into the most strategic position where it would have the greatest effect. General Washington, after spending almost the entire war running away from the British to keep his ragtag army together, moved heaven and earth to get his troops into position for a long-awaited strike against Cornwallis. Washington understood that a win at Yorktown could be the critical turning point of the war. *Everything* hinged on this battle.

Understanding and Application

Blaming the loss of the Battle of the Bay entirely on Admiral Graves misses a larger point. Any number of the British commanders, both land and naval, could have figured out what Admiral Rodney suspected from his post in the Caribbean. Cornwallis could have squirmed his way out of the impending trap at Yorktown and avoided the siege altogether. And had he done so, it's probable that the British would ultimately have won the war. In fact, it's an absolute miracle that the American colonists won the Revolutionary War against the most powerful empire in the world.

But they *did* win the war. And they did so in large part because they succeeded at concentrating their forces where it mattered most at one critical moment. Without the win at Yorktown, an entirely different outcome could have resulted.

Likewise, leaders today can win strategic battles, and ultimately the war, by concentrating their focus, energy, and resources where they matter most. This requires an understanding of the difference between strategy and tactics. Strategy determines *what* you're trying to accomplish. Tactics are *how* you accomplish your objective. It's easy to blame Graves's loss of the Battle of the Bay on his poor tactics. But ultimately, the battle was lost because of a poor overall British strategy and an effective American/French strategy.

By concentrating forces in the execution of wise strategy, leaders are able to beat superior forces. They overcome their own weaknesses and deficiencies to exploit those of their competitors.

Illustration #2: George Anson at the Battle of Cape Finisterre

In 1744, the Royal Navy had suffered humiliation during a skirmish with a combined French and Spanish fleet off the coast of Toulon. After the battle, a court-martial was called and the fleet commander and nine other captains involved were dismissed. In July 1746, in the wake of the Toulon affair, Vice-Admiral George Anson was named as commander of the Western Squadron for the Royal Navy. His responsibilities were as daunting as they were myriad: protecting the English Channel; blockading Brest; and intercepting any French detachments or convoys sailing from any of the Biscay ports to the Americas, the Mediterranean, or the Far East.

To fulfill his responsibilities, it would have made sense for Anson to disperse his fleet across the Bay of Biscay, from Ushant on the northwestern tip of France to Cape Finisterre on the northwestern tip of Spain. But Anson, aggressive and eager to erase the humiliation of Toulon, was not about to go on the defensive. Instead, he sought immediate battle with the French.

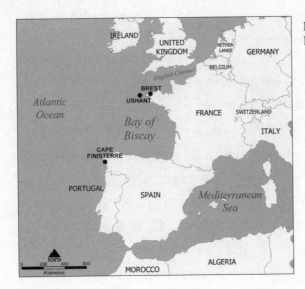

Figure 6: Map of Bay of Biscay

On May 3, 1747, while sailing off Cape Finisterre, Anson's squadron of sixteen ships, which carried a total of 938 guns, encountered a weaker French squadron of fifteen warships carrying a total of 552 guns and escorting a convoy of thirty-eight merchantmen. Anson immediately sent up the signal to chase the French to close the distance between the two fleets. The French commander signaled his fleet to retire, and once again, Anson went on the chase. After a swift and decisive battle, Anson's ships had captured the entire French squadron and eighteen of the thirty-eight merchantmen.

Given the Royal Navy's superiority in firing power, the outcome seemed inevitable. But this ignores the fact that the only reason Anson had the superior force was because he had not divided his fleet in a defensive posture, which, as Michael A. Palmer explained, "a commander of lesser caliber" might have easily done. Instead, Palmer further explains, "...Anson, on his own initiative, kept the bulk of his force concentrated and applied his strength at the right place and at the right time."[2]

Understanding and Application

Anson was charged with a difficult task—to achieve a wide variety of objectives with a relatively small force. All of the objectives were necessary; none could be neglected or compromised. Most commanders would have scattered their fleet to concurrently attempt to achieve the objectives. But in an effort to achieve many objectives, they wouldn't have been able to achieve any of them; scattering forces would have made them weak on every front. Anson's best tactic to achieve the strategy of protecting a variety of fronts was, counter-intuitively, to concentrate his forces.

Leaders today face a similar dilemma: multiple worthy objectives competing for their attention. The logical thing to do in this situation is to disperse one's time, energy, and resources across all fronts. But more often than not, this is a losing tactic. Many times, the most effective way to achieve multiple objectives is to concentrate all your energy on one key strategy, one critical objective.

This requires a leader to prioritize. Effective prioritization can only occur when a leader thinks through actions and weighs consequences. He or she has to see the big picture to understand how one decision impacts the whole. Like a chess player, the leader has to understand what events will unfold by making one move and has to see several moves into the future. He or she has to understand when it makes sense to sacrifice a bishop in order to capture the queen and always has to keep in mind the overarching objective to checkmate the king, rather than focusing all his or her attention on protecting one pawn.

If you pick the one right objective to concentrate on, the other objectives naturally fall into place.

Illustration #3: The Battle of the Nile

In the spring of 1798, Napoleon contrived a top-secret plan to cripple Britain. The French Directory had struggled with finding a way to challenge the Royal Navy (which remained firmly in control of the Atlantic Ocean) at sea. The French navy, however, was dominant in the Mediterranean, the British fleet having withdrawn after a war with Spain in 1796. Rather than confronting Britain directly, Napoleon proposed an invasion of Egypt. By establishing a base in Egypt, he conjectured, the French would have a staging point to take on British India, which was an essential part of the British empire. By severing Britain's connection with India, France could effectively eliminate the primary source of wealth allowing Britain to continue the war.

The French Directory agreed with Napoleon's plan, and he assembled more than 35,000 soldiers and developed a powerful fleet at Toulon, on the French Mediterranean. He also formed a body of scientists and engineers who would be used to establish a French colony in Egypt. Napoleon kept their destination secret and did not reveal his ultimate goal until after the first stage of the expedition was complete.

On May 19, 1798, Bonaparte's armada set sail from Toulon, stopping at various locations en route to gather more troops and supplies. While passing through to Egypt, the French conquered the island of Malta, resupplied, and continued their expedition, arriving off the coast of Alexandria on June 29.

When the French fleet crossed the Mediterranean, Rear-Admiral Sir Horatio Nelson was sent to discover Bonaparte's intentions and destroy his fleet. The British fleet chased the French for two months, narrowly missing them on a number of occasions. It was one of the greatest cat-and-mouse games ever played.

After capturing Alexandria in a brief battle, Bonaparte led the main force of his army inland. He instructed his naval commander, Vice-Admiral Brueys, to anchor in the Alexandria harbor, where he could assist Napoleon from sea. But the channel into the harbor was too narrow and shallow, so Brueys chose instead to anchor at Aboukir Bay, twenty miles northeast of Alexandria. There, he placed his fleet into a formidable defensive position, lining the ships up across the bay, their starboard sides facing the sea, and connecting them together with cables. The 120-gun flagship, *L'Orient*, was placed in the center. The French felt confident in their position, believing that no ships could break the line and sail behind them because of the shallowness of the harbor and the danger of ships grounding on the shoals. They were certain that a British attack would follow the line ahead procedure, with each ship following in a line and sailing across the French formation on the seaward side. With this confidence, the French only prepared their cannons on the starboard side.

On August 1, after a long and frustrating chase, Nelson arrived at Alexandria and finally discovered the position of the French fleet. He immediately turned his own toward Aboukir Bay and arrived there in late afternoon of that same day. The stage was set. Both the French and British forces were concentrated on one critical point. Whoever won this battle would tip the scales in the war. By all appearances, the French held the advantage. Their position appeared to be impregnable. The two fleets were almost equal in number—the French had thirteen battleships against Nelson's fifteen—but the French had more and larger firepower.

Nelson knew that attacking would be a huge risk and that his fleet would undoubtedly sustain horrible damage and losses. But his philosophy, as he later wrote, was that "difficulties and dangers but increase my desire of attempting them."[3] With both forces concentrated, it all came down to who was more prepared and who could win the advantage. Nelson felt confident in his captains and sailors.

When the British fleet sailed into the bay, many of the French soldiers were on land gathering food and water. Even after seeing the British sails, they did not hasten back to their ships, believing, incorrectly, that the British would not attack until morning. But when Nelson ordered an immediate attack, they scrambled back to their ships.

The French had concentrated, anchored, and prepared their fleet for battle but with a glaring weak spot: they had left enough room for ships to pass between the front of their fleet and the shore. Captain Foley, commander of the British ship *Goliath*, observed this and daringly led several ships around the French fleet to the shore side, where the French had not prepared their cannons.

The French ships at the front and middle of the line were trapped in a crossfire and battered on both sides by British ships, while the Frenchmen in the ships anchored at the end of the line could but watch helplessly from the sidelines. Even the ships engaged in battle were only half engaged, not having prepared to fire toward the port (shore) side. After a fierce three-hour battle, the leading French warships surrendered. The center withstood the initial British attack.

When reinforcements arrived, the French ships were assaulted again. Just before ten o'clock that night, the French flagship *L'Orient* caught fire and exploded—with such tremendous force that it was heard fifteen miles away in Alexandria. The shock of the eruption and resulting carnage was so horrific that it actually caused the raging battle to cease, as if the combatants had been frozen in place. It was a spontaneous cease-fire that lasted for several pregnant minutes. The fighting would continue, but the tragic obliteration of France's most treasured flagship marked the beginning of the end.

Figure 7: The Battle of the Nile: Destruction of *L'Orient* 1 August 1798 by Mather Brown, National Maritime Museum

The French commander, Brueys, had been killed in battle. With their vanguard and center defeated, the rear division attempted to escape the bay, but the British captured all but two ships of the line and two frigates from a total of seventeen ships engaged—an unheard of, lopsided tally.

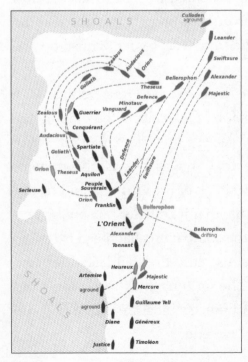

Figure 8: Map of ship positions and movements during the Battle of Aboukir Bay, 1–2 August 1798. The map has been simplified and differs from the text.

The British victory was overwhelming. Ten ships of the French fleet had been burned, sunk, or captured, while *Nelson had not lost a single ship*. British casualties were estimated at 218, with 677 wounded, while the French lost an estimated 5,235 sailors, with 3,305 taken prisoner. The next morning, after surveying the utter devastation, Nelson wrote, "Victory is not a name strong enough for such a scene."[4] The battle was a pivotal point in the war with the French. Bonaparte's army was now effectively trapped in Egypt. The Royal Navy thereafter asserted dominance in the Mediterranean, and this dominance contributed significantly to the French defeat at the Siege of Acre the following year that proved to be the downfall of Napoleon's dream of an eastern empire. Nelson, who had been wounded in the battle, was lauded as a hero and received a shower of prizes and praise. (Interestingly, one strange prize he received was a coffin made from the mast of the French flagship *L'Orient*, which had exploded in the battle. Nelson was buried in this coffin in St. Paul's Cathedral after being killed during the Battle of Trafalgar.)

Understanding and Application

The Battle of the Nile is a graphic case study in concentration. Both the French and the British were concentrating their forces where it mattered. Napoleon was a master of strategic concentration. His strategy to avoid a direct confrontation with Britain and instead invade Egypt was brilliant. Had he succeeded in cutting off Britain's connection with India, he likely would have crippled its ability to continue waging the war. He made the right strategic decision and concentrated his forces in the right place at the right time.

French Admiral Brueys also concentrated his fleet strategically to protect his inland troops. Unfortunately for him, he didn't plan well enough and left an Achilles' heel wide open for the British. Nelson was also a master of concentration. He knew how critical the battle was. He was fully aware of the consequences if he lost — and the opportunity if he won. He and his captains were able to concentrate their forces on the weak spot of the French fleet and take advantage of it.

One key difference to the outcome of that battle was that Nelson understood it to be an absolute vital priority to win. Judging by Brueys's failure to properly prepare, we can only surmise that his commitment to protecting the bay was outmatched by Nelson's obsessive focus on taking it. Once Nelson found the French, he did not hesitate, equivocate, or falter. He did not worry about the distinct possibility of the concentrated fleets destroying each other. His resolve, based on his priority, was unwavering. He was determined to win the battle no matter the cost.

Leaders can learn much from this example. It's not just enough to concentrate your forces in one strategic area; you also must be 100 percent committed to winning the battle in that area. You must attack immediately and relentlessly, not only concentrating your forces but *committing* them. You must charge the hill and win the strategic battleground.

Summary

Ineffective prioritization is often a greater weakness for leaders than poor decision making. In an attempt to win too many battles on too many fronts, leaders often lose the war.

One of the most critical roles leaders play is to pick the right battles in the right places at the right time. A key component of effective strategy is prioritization: learning when, where, and how to concentrate one's energy and resources. A strategic plan is useless without a hierarchy of priorities. It's not enough to just know what to do; leaders must also know in what order to do things. Furthermore, leaders must know what *not* to do and where *not* to focus their efforts.

Effective leaders focus their efforts, energy, and resources on one paramount objective. They obsess over that objective. They go around, over, under, or through any obstacle in their path to achieving that objective. By concentrating their forces on one strategic battle at a time, they can ultimately win the war.

CHAPTER SEVEN

The Lesson of Decentralization

Leadership Principle:

Effective leadership is not about getting subordinates to follow your orders promptly and to the letter. Rather, it's about empowering people to rise up to leadership themselves. It's about entrusting them with decisions and helping them grow. It's about encouraging them to take initiative.

Stereotypical, military-style, command-and-control leaders can never duplicate their efforts and multiply their effectiveness; since they have to be the one calling all the shots, they have to be physically present to make anything happen. Command-and-control leadership creates a culture of fear and hesitancy. As a result, followers don't take initiative for fear of being reprimanded or punished.

In contrast, effective leaders don't mold obedient followers, but rather they develop confident leaders. Good leaders trust their people. They communicate well with them. They develop them intentionally. Instead of creating robots who act the same way, they create a culture of like-minded people based on shared ideals and principles.

Illustration #1: The "Nelson Touch" at the Battle of the Nile

In the last chapter, we featured Nelson's overwhelming victory at the Battle of the Nile and focused on the lesson of concentration. But there's more to that story that we haven't discussed yet. When Nelson sailed into Aboukir Bay, he was certain that his fleet could win — though he did not know exactly how. The customary approach would have been to stop and create a battle plan and wait until morning to execute it. But Nelson was far from the typical commander. He ordered an immediate attack and charged full speed ahead, "relying on his captains to use their initiative,"[1] as Roy and Lesley Adkins wrote.

The first ship to arrive in battle position was the *Goliath*, commanded by Captain Thomas Foley. Foley observed that the French ships were only anchored at the bow, which meant that there must be a strip of deep water between the ships and the shallows. (Otherwise, the ships would have had to have been anchored at both bow and stern.) Foley's aide-de-camp, Midshipman Elliot, wrote that, as he was standing close to Captain Foley, "I heard him say to the master that he wished he could get inside of the leading ship of the enemy's line....I also heard Foley say, he should not be surprised to find the Frenchmen unprepared for action on the inner side."[2] Acting on his own initiative and needing no order from Nelson to break the protocol of the line, Foley steered his ship around the first French ship in the line, the *Guerrier*, and came up on its port side. Just as he had suspected, the French ship was unprepared to fire on the harbor-facing side. Captain Hood followed Foley, as did a number of other British ships.

The British were thus able to surround and pummel the French from both sides and destroy almost their entire fleet.

Understanding and Application

The stunning British victory at the Battle of the Nile can largely be attributed to one thing: the principle of decentralization. Arthur Herman writes that Nelson was not bothered by the fact that he did not know how to win the battle when he ordered the attack because he had learned from previous battles that:

> ...no admiral, no matter how organized or enterprising, could control the action and tempo of a sea battle from his quarterdeck. The pace was too fast, the noise and smoke too distracting, the sudden opportunities too fleeting, and the system of signaling and communicating with his fleet too primitive, to allow him to plan and plot each move and countermove. The best an admiral could do was devise his strategy, point his ships in the right direction, and trust his captains to carry out his plan as they, not he, saw fit in the heat and smoke of battle. "I was

sure each would feel for a French ship," was how Nelson put it, and that was all he wanted.

His confidence and trust in his captains sprang from the other crucial lesson he had learned....A commander's subordinates had to understand not just *what* he was planning to do, but *why*.[3]

Long before the battle ever took place, Nelson had discussed his plans with all his captains for how to engage with a French fleet in precisely such an anchored position. Therefore, Herman writes, "This team of trusted officers came to understand his strategic thinking almost as well as he did."[4] Hence, a pre-battle conference was not necessary.

Nathan Miller adds:

All the elements of what became known as the "Nelson Touch" were clearly visible at the Battle of the Nile: inspiring leadership, the intensive training of his captains, the delegation of crucial tactical decisions to them in the heat of battle rather than slavish adherence to the *Fighting Instructions*, and the taking of calculated risks to ensure that a battle would be not only decisive but devastating to an enemy fleet.[5]

The Battle of the Nile was won the moment Captain Thomas Foley, having been trained and empowered by Nelson to make judgment calls in the heat of battle, broke from protocol to sail around the French line and attack from the harbor side. Rather than trying to control every little detail of the battle himself, Nelson trained his commanding officers well. He taught them guiding principles and then fully expected them to act on their own initiative to make the right decisions under fire. The British were able to surprise the French and attack immediately, with no battle conference, because Nelson had decentralized command through proper training.

Leaders focus on training their people *before* battle rather than ordering them *during* battle. They then trust their people to take initiative and make decisions, even if it means breaking from protocol. Success is less dependent on hard work and knowledge than it is the ability to lead people. Nelson didn't have complete knowledge on how to defeat the French at Aboukir Bay. But what he did have was the ability to lead. His leadership, not his knowledge, made all the difference at the Battle of the Nile.

Illustration # 2: Suffren's Indian Ocean Campaign

What Admiral Horatio Nelson was to the British, Admiral Pierre André de Suffren was to the French. When Napoleon himself learned during his exile of Suffren's exploits, he bemoaned, "Why did he not live until my time? Why could I not find someone of his kind? I should have made him my Nelson and our affairs would have taken a very different turn. Instead I spent all my time looking for such a sailor and never found one." Although possessed by "demonic energy, frenetic impatience, [and] uncontrolled fury," as one biographer wrote, Suffren was a brilliant strategist and tactician. His execution, however, was lacking.[6]

In 1781, after serving thirty-eight years in the naval service, he received a commission to command the French fleet in the Indian Ocean. From his experience and from studying historical works detailing the exploits of the great Dutch admiral de Ruyter, Suffren wrote an assessment of the French navy and concluded that its strategic and tactical methods "resulted in the paralysis of the spirit of audacity, intelligent response, support under fire, and the camaraderie of combat." He felt that the way the French handled their fleet during the American war was full of "idiotic maneuvers," "stupid, perfidious counsels," and "lost opportunities." (Other than that, he didn't feel strongly about it!) He chafed under order and preferred captains to act on their own initiative during battle, much the same as Nelson would later do.[7]

His orders were to protect French colonial possessions in the ocean and support France's allies in the region. He set sail, a maverick determined to play by his own rules, with the "spirit of initiative." He believed that the best way to achieve his objectives was to go on the offensive and seek and destroy the British squadron, which required an aggressive handling of the fleet. Even though his captains were "accustomed to the rigid discipline of the line, where they waited for signals," Suffren "demanded initiative" from them.[8]

Over the next two years, he fought half a dozen battles. In each of them, he struggled to get his captains to fulfill his strategy: seize the initiative and concentrate their entire squadron against part of the enemy's. In February 1783, he engaged in battle against British Vice-Admiral Sir Edward Hughes. Suffren attacked, but his commanders failed to support him, and the engagement broke off with neither side losing a ship. This pattern repeated itself on four subsequent occasions.

Michael A. Palmer writes:

While his strategy was sound and his tactical proclivities admirable, he was unable to fully execute his ideas. Time and again he was dissatisfied with, and often infuriated by, the lack of support from his subordinates. But why did he go unsupported? Suffren's biographer concluded that he "failed to ensure that his captains knew what was expected of them." He looked for displays of initiative from men who had only the vaguest understanding of their commander's tactical ideas, ideas that were a marked departure from French naval doctrine. Suffren expected far too much from men who not only failed to measure up to their British counterparts but also were not among the best and brightest of the French navy. "By the time Suffren came to fight his last battle," Cavaliero wrote, "he had learnt that only time-honoured tactics would do for sailors as he commanded."[9]

177

Understanding and Application

Although Suffren's strategy, which worked phenomenally well for Nelson, was sound, unlike Nelson, he failed to intentionally develop his captains. He expected them to take initiative without adequately training them to make good decisions. His expectations were not backed by communication.

It's not enough as a leader to simply expect initiative on the part of your people. You have to train and develop them. You have to communicate with them so they know what you expect. The most important role of a leader, which should take the bulk of his or her time, is to develop other leaders. True leaders don't just act boldly themselves and expect others to follow; they teach others how to decide and act boldly and rightly as well.

Illustration #3: Mathews at the Battle of Toulon

Between 1740 and 1748, most of Europe was engaged in the War of the Austrian Succession, with Austria, Britain, and the Dutch Republic allied on one side and France, Spain, and Prussia allied with the Electorate of Bavaria. In 1741, Britain officially declared war against Spain, and war with France was imminent. Thomas Mathews, after seven years of retirement, was given command of the Royal Navy squadron in the Mediterranean. His second-in-command was Rear-Admiral Richard Lestock, a man with whom Mathews was not on good terms.

In December of 1743, the British were warily watching Spanish and French squadrons anchored at Toulon.

France, though informally allied against the British, had not formally declared war. But Mathews had received intelligence indicating that France was preparing to enter the war. On February 9, the combined Franco-Spanish force, consisting of twenty-eight ships of the line, set sail from Toulon. Mathews, eager to engage them, pursued.

In the chase, the British fleet became scattered in light winds. On February 22, Mathews signaled for the formation of the line of battle. By nightfall, the line had not been formed yet. By morning, the fleet was still scattered too far apart to mount an attack, despite Mathews's signals. Lestock, commanding the rear, was slow to respond. The enemy ships pulled away as the British simply tried to get organized. Mathews, fearing that the French and Spanish ships would escape and join the French force gathered at Brest for the planned invasion of Britain, was desperate to attack. When the Spanish ships fell behind the French, Mathews decided to attack their rear, despite his fleet being separated and disorganized.

He hoisted the signal to attack and left the line to attack the Spanish rear followed by one other British ship, the HMS *Marlborough* captained by James Cornewall. Unfortunately, his signal to form the line of battle was still left flying. The other British captains were confused by the two signals flying simultaneously. They were further confused by the unusual attack, which broke protocol. They were forced to choose between reading Mathews's mind (to concentrate forces and strike a quick knockout blow to the Spanish ships at the rear) or following the standard

Fighting Instructions and pursuing other Spanish ships in the middle and at the front.

Outnumbered and unsupported, the other commanders too uncertain to engage, Mathews and Cornewall successfully engaged with the enemy but suffered considerable damage. When the French ships turned around to aid the Spanish, with no orders from Mathews and being utterly confused by the lack of instructions, the British captains broke the line and fled to the northwest. Britain viewed the battle as a crushing defeat—an embarrassing fiasco created by indecisiveness and disorganization. Mathews, Lestock, and eleven other captains were court-martialed. Mathews, charged with bringing the fleet into action in a disorganized manner, fleeing the enemy, and failing to bring the enemy into action when the conditions were advantageous, was dismissed from the navy, along with nine captains.

Understanding and Application

Like Suffren's maverick ideas, Mathews's strategy was actually quite excellent. He was willing to break from protocol to deal with specific circumstances. Had his other commanders simply known what he wanted to do, the result could have been drastically different. As it turned out, Mathews was thoroughly castigated for deviating from the accepted norms of battle.

But the truth is that Mathews failed not by straying from the line but by failing to train and communicate with his captains. The first charge brought against him in his court-martial was that he did not hold any councils of war or any other meetings with his commanders, either routinely or before the battle. Unlike Nelson before the Battle of the Nile, Mathews never discussed possibilities of battle with his subordinates. They had no idea what he expected of them and what he was trying to accomplish. As one biographer wrote, "Mathews was to blame for not keeping his captains generally informed about the situation. There is no sign that he discussed tactical questions with them."[10]

The second charge leveled against him was that he had not trained his fleet on additional signals and instructions. It was common practice for admirals to issue their own instructions, in addition to the standard *Fighting Instructions*, to direct commanders during battle. Despite having commanded in the Mediterranean for two years before the battle of Toulon, Mathews had developed no such personalized system of communication.

Yes, leaders must lead by example. But that doesn't mean they can expect people to read their minds. In addition to setting the example, communication is vital to leadership. It's easy to believe that overcommunicating with people can sap their initiative. But the truth is exactly the opposite: the more a leader communicates, the better his people understand his intentions, strategies, and objectives and the more empowered they are to assist in their fulfillment.

Summary

Among the greatest enemies of leadership are blind following, created by centralized bureaucracy, and hesitancy on the part of team members, created by a style of command and control. The most effective teams are those that are led not by strict rules but by guiding principles, not by dictates but by inspiration and empowerment.

Effective leaders empower their people and multiply their efforts by trusting their people, communicating well with them, and intentionally developing them. They also unite people around shared values, ideals, and principles, which take the place of strict and myriad rules that are expected to be obeyed mindlessly. Effective leaders don't want blind followers but confident leaders who take initiative and make good decisions autonomously. The best thing that can be said about a leader is not that people follow him but that there are more leaders because of his training, guidance, and development.

A team led by such a leader is courageous, innovative, and nimble. New ideas are constantly generated by every member of the team and encouraged and appreciated by the leader. When threats arise, adjustments are made quickly and spontaneously. When chaos reigns, when the smoke of battle is thick, team members act on their own initiative to solve problems. In contrast, a team that is led by a dictator or a poor communicator is fearful, stagnant, and hesitant. New ideas are squashed and ignored. The team is slow to adapt to change and is often overcome by it.

In short, the most effective team is one that is decentralized and empowered by a good leader.

CHAPTER EIGHT

The Lesson of Culture

Leadership Principle:

Few things give leaders more leverage and cause more impact than developing culture. Culture is the combination of values, traditions, ideals, aspirations, and principles that determine what a team or organization stands for—and stands against. Culture says, "This is who we are. This is how we act. This is how we do things here. And this is how we do not do things here." When a culture is properly instilled, leaders no longer have to dictate from the top; team members get an intuitive feel for what is expected of them. Rather, their role is to hold people accountable to the shared culture and continue fanning the flames of inspiration.

Leaders must develop a culture of victory—a culture that says, "Here, we are winners. We will prevail. We will not be distracted or deterred from our mission. *Nothing* can stop us from succeeding." Leaders are obsessed with winning. They keep score. They are constantly adjusting and adapting to changing circumstances and threats in order to achieve their objective. They stay fixated upon their North Star and sail in an undeviating course toward it, using their sails and rudders to adjust to the wind and waves.

This relentless focus bleeds down into the lowest ranks. In a well-cultivated culture, the lowest people in the trenches are animated, encouraged, and emboldened by the shared identity. They need not be hounded, prodded, or micro-managed; they take pride in their work and strive to live up to the cultural values and ideals. One of the most critical things a leader can do, therefore, is to communicate and cultivate a culture of confidence.

Illustration #1: Nelson versus Villeneuve at the Battle of Trafalgar

In 1805, during the War of the Third Coalition of the Napoleonic Wars, France was dominant in Europe on land, while the Royal Navy remained firmly in control of the seas. Napoleon was determined to invade Britain. To do so, he would need to control the English Channel—a monumental feat given the Royal Navy's power and sheer numbers. The main French fleets were stationed at Brest in Brittany and Toulon on the Mediterranean, with allied Spanish fleets waiting to help in Cádiz and Ferrol in northern Spain. The British were blockading the French and Spanish fleets, with Nelson stationed at Toulon. Napoleon's plan was to have them break the blockade and join forces in the Caribbean, where they would jointly clear the channel to make way for the invasion.

The French fleet at Toulon, under Nelson's counterpart, Admiral Pierre-Charles Villeneuve, was able to evade Nelson's blockade when the British were blown out to sea by storms. Villeneuve passed through the Strait of Gibraltar and rendezvoused with the Spanish fleet, eventually ending up in Cádiz, off the southwestern coast of Spain. Meanwhile, on August 15, Admiral Cornwallis, stationed to protect the English Channel, decided to send twenty of his ships of the line to engage the enemy forces in Spain. This fleet, commanded by Vice-Admiral Calder, reached Cádiz on September 15, and Nelson arrived there to take command on September 29.

The British were forced to sail south to Gibraltar to replenish their supplies. The French and Spanish remained in Cádiz awaiting orders. On October 20, the combined French and Spanish fleet left Cádiz and sailed south toward Gibraltar. That evening, they spotted British ships of the line in pursuit and prepared for battle. During the night, they were ordered into a single line. The next day, they spotted Nelson's fleet of twenty-seven ships of the line pursuing them from the northwest with the wind behind it. A fearful and hesitant Villeneuve ordered his fleet into three columns but then changed his mind, which resulted in an uneven formation.

At 6:00 a.m. that morning, off the Cape of Trafalgar, Nelson ordered his men to prepare for battle. At 8:00 a.m.,

Villenueve ordered his fleet to turn around and return to Cádiz. Under a light and shifting wind, it took the ships an hour and a half to complete his order, and they were formed in an uneven, angular crescent. By 11:00 a.m. Villeneuve could see Nelson's entire fleet, which was formed in two parallel columns, a highly unusual formation. According to the prevailing orthodoxy of the time, as we've discussed, Nelson should have approached the enemy in a single line of battle and then engaged them broadside in parallel lines. But his plan was to attack in two columns, sailing perpendicular to the enemy's line to split it into three parts. Once divided, Nelson's fleet could surround one third and destroy it. This plan would create a mêlée, with a series of individual ship-to-ship battles, which Nelson was confident his commanders would win. It would also prevent the van of Villeneuve's fleet from being able to turn around in time to help.

The British were the inferior force, their 17,000 men and 2,148 guns competing with the enemy's 30,000 men and 2,568 guns. The Franco-Spanish fleet also had six more ships of the line than the British, which meant they could combine their fire and gang up on individual British ships. But Nelson and his commanders had been preparing for this battle for months and were supremely confident in the outcome. Wrote one sailor, "During this momentous preparation, the human mind had ample time for meditation and conjecture, for it was evident that the fate of England rested on this battle."[1]

Nelson led the windward column in the *Victory*, with Admiral Collingwood leading the leeward column in the *Royal Sovereign*. Just before his column engaged the enemy, Collingwood said to his officers, "Now, gentlemen, let us do something today which the world may talk of hereafter."[2]

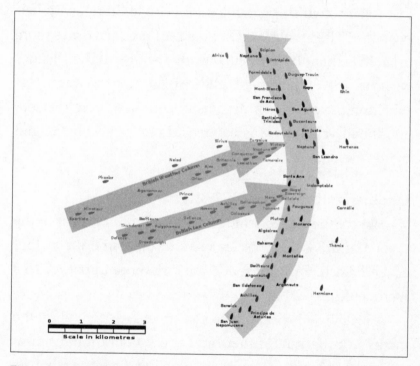

Figure 9: Situation at noon as the British broke into the Franco-Spanish line

The first shots were fired at noon. Because of their perpendicular position, the British ships were under heavy fire for almost an hour before they could bring their own guns to bear. But once they were in position, the battle was fierce and chaotic. Early in the battle, Nelson was struck by a musket bullet in the left shoulder, which passed through his spine. He exclaimed, "They finally succeeded; I am dead!"[3] and was carried below decks. He died three hours after being hit, but not before murmuring, "Thank God I have done my duty."[4] The British forged on. One by one, French and Spanish ships began surrendering.

When the smoke cleared, the Franco-Spanish fleet had lost twenty-two ships, while not a single British ship had been lost! The French and Spanish suffered ten times more casualties than the British. Despite the loss of their leader early in the engagement, the British victory was overwhelming. Napoleon's dreams of conquest were dashed, and the Royal Navy was never again seriously challenged by the French.

Understanding and Application

The combined technological force and firepower of the French and Spanish navies were in fact superior to that of the British. So what made the difference in battle? In a word, culture.

A British sailor explained the effect Nelson had on the men: "…in fighting under him, every man thought himself sure of success."[5] Another sailor, Lieutenant Senhouse, added, "The mode of attack, adopted with such success in the Trafalgar action, appears to me to have succeeded from the enthusiasm inspired throughout the British fleet from their being commanded by their beloved Nelson."[6]

In contrast, one of Villeneuve's captains complained to his officers before the Battle of Trafalgar, "The fleet is doomed. The French admiral does not know his business."[7] It's doubtful that Villeneuve himself would have disagreed; he was afraid of Nelson and had little confidence that the French could defeat him. He had fought at the Battle of the Nile and had experienced crushing defeat at the hand of Nelson. He knew that his men were not nearly as well-trained as Nelson's, but this was essentially an excuse to cover his own lack of confidence and failure of nerve. As Arthur Herman wrote, "At the end of the day, Villeneuve believed no matter what he did, Nelson would win....In a crucial sense, he had lost the Battle of Trafalgar the very day he took command."[8]

The French fleet was, indeed, doomed from the beginning—though certainly not because of any lack of ships, firepower, or men. Adam Nicolson explained:

The asymmetry between British confidence and Franco-Spanish despair, at the very beginning of the battle, is the governing condition of Trafalgar. The battle was lost and won before a moment of it was fought....The French and Spanish commanders knew, as if it were their destiny, that a catastrophe awaited them.

In light of this, what happened at Trafalgar is, on one level, not complicated: a highly ambitious, confident and aggressive English battle fleet found and attacked a larger combined French and Spanish fleet whose morale was broken, whose command was divided and without conviction, and heavily defeated it....In some ways, that was all: a pack of dogs battened on to a flock of sheep....

Technology does not distinguish the fleets—or at least not sufficiently. What makes them different are the people on board. Trafalgar is a meeting of men. It is in the men that the difference lies between aggression and the need to defend; between the desire to attack and destroy and the desperate fear for one's life; between the ability to persist in battle when surrounded by gore, grief and destruction and the need to submit to the natural instincts to surrender...[9]

Arthur Herman added, "Villeneuve and his men were fighting for the sake of honor; Nelson's men were fighting to win."[10]

The culture of winning inspired by Nelson, not any tactical superiority, was the deciding factor at Trafalgar. In fact, as Adam Nicolson wrote, "The [British] tactics were immensely weak. The success depended on the independent ferocity and fighting aggression of each British ship and on the example of leadership given by Nelson to his captains."[11]

Illustration #2: Hawke versus Conflans at the Battle of Quiberon Bay

Nelson was not the only British admiral to inspire confidence. Much earlier, Admiral Hawke, who earned his fame at the Battle of Quiberon in 1759, was cut from the same cloth. We discussed that battle in chapter three, focusing on Hawke's innovative blockade. But it was more than his blockade that led to an eventual victory at Quiberon Bay against French Admiral Conflans.

One sailor, Augustus Hervey, left us a clue into the kind of culture Hawke created. Shortly after Hawke took over the Western Squadron, some three years before the Battle at Quiberon Bay, he addressed his senior captains. Hervey wrote that Hawke "made us a fine speech that he was determined to run close up to [the French], and that the honour of our country required we should do our very utmost to destroy these ships and he did not doubt that we should, with a great deal of all this sort of stuff."[12]

Hawke lived true to his bold words. His confidence and aggressiveness, which were unmatched by any French admiral, were passed on to his crews. Historian Brian Tunstall noted that by the time Hawke's fleet faced Conflans at Quiberon Bay after the blockade, "Hawke's captains had developed such a highly aggressive spirit throughout the long blockade that they did not require special signals to urge them on."[13] In short, while the French were desperate to avoid battle with Hawke, Hawke and his crew were eager to engage.

In fact, the battle was prefaced by Conflans trying to escape the British by sailing into the bay, for which Hawke had no charts, in violent weather. He was gambling that the British would dare not follow for fear of running into the rocks. But Conflans vastly underestimated Hawke. Hawke wrote, "Monsieur Conflans kept going off under such sail as all his squadron could carry, and at the same time keep together; while we crowded after him with every sail our ships could bear."[14] Arthur Herman wrote:

> In contrast to his French counterpart, Hawke had confidence in his sailors and their seamanship. He had confidence that his officers...would fight the way Hawke liked — as quickly and as closely as possible. Above all, he was confident that if he fought the French, regardless of the weather, he would win.[15]

Understanding and Application

Nelson and Hawke both inspired confidence in their men. But they did so not just through words but also through their actions. Their words may have been inspiring, but their actions made them real and believable.

Credibility, then, is the bedrock of confidence. Words, if backed by actions, can inspire people to great achievement. But when they are not backed by actions, they are mere platitudes, which are ignored and even mocked. The confidence or timidity of a leader is transferred to his troops less through his words than through his actions. Hawke talked a big game when he took over command, and he proved his words by taking immediate, bold, and courageous action. When he spoke, his men listened; they knew he meant what he said. Great leaders create confidence by backing up their inspiring words with valiant action.

194

They also intentionally build high morale. They have high emotional intelligence and are in tune with the thoughts and emotions of their troops. They spend time with their people in the trenches to understand what's happening and what's being felt on the ground. They demonstrate, through thoughtful words and considerate actions, that they care about their people. They make a thorough study of other people's needs and know what their people value. They recognize the contributions of others. They don't hog the spotlight for themselves but constantly shine it on other people. They don't shame or criticize; they edify and compliment.

Just as Nelson's and Hawke's men followed them eagerly into battle, your people will too when they trust you, when they have confidence in your leadership, and when they feel that you value them.

Illustration #3: The Culture of the English Navy versus the French Navy

In truth, more than the contributions of any individual officer, the confident culture of the Royal Navy was driven by an unavoidable reality. In 1756, an English author explained, "The moment we lose our Dominion of the Sea, we cease to exist."[16] This was at the core of the Royal Navy's culture, which determined its dominance throughout the age of fighting sail. For Britons, sea power was a matter of national mission and myth—because it was a matter of grim survival. Poems were written of naval heroes, elevating them to the status of legends. Newspapers lauded their fame. The fame of today's celebrities and sports stars pales in comparison to that of British naval officers.

In contrast, for the French, sea power was seen simply as a complement to land power. Hence, their navy consistently floundered, often finding itself short on money, men, resources, and training, while the Royal Navy was consistently well-funded, well-armed, and well-trained. As Arthur Herman wrote, "...for all its skill and brilliance, the French navy had no staying power. French governments simply were never under the same political pressures, the same passionate public dedication, to having a navy second to none that British governments faced."[17] This "passionate public dedication" bred an almost irrational confidence in British seamen, which was never equaled by the French.

One would think that the supreme confidence of the British would have led to overconfidence, therefore causing them to slack off, and that the lack of confidence on the part of the French would have spurred them to frantic action. In fact, it was just the opposite: the British were confident precisely because they trained and prepared relentlessly, while the French were lackadaisical in their training. As Herman wrote, "While Napoleon's ships sat largely idle in harbor, British crews and officers had been standing on and off for the better part of a decade, constantly at the ready with continuous drills and gunnery practice."[18] In short, the British stayed hungry.

There are other, deeper reasons why the British were hungry "dogs" and the French were complacent "sheep."

Their naval cultures were each a reflection of social structure. In England, naval officers came from a broad spectrum of society, stretching from the aristocracy to the lowest classes. In fact, military service was seen as the one place where lower classes could raise their position in society. In France, however, only aristocrats were eligible to be officers. British seamen could rise through the ranks based on their merit; French seamen were allowed no such privilege. Undoubtedly, this meant that British vessels were captained by officers who had earned their position, while French naval officers may not have been the most qualified for the job.[19]

Tellingly, after the French Revolution, the French navy swung to the opposite side of the scale, from rigid aristocracy to egalitarian democracy. As Herman wrote:

The revolution had shattered the old French navy. The majority of sea officers, the aristocrats of the old *Grand Corps*, had quit or fled France. A century-old tradition of naval skill and excellence vanished. Ideological correctness took its place. The revolution abolished the "undemocratic" rank of master gunner — fatally weakening the French navy's firepower right down to Trafalgar — and offered captaincies to anyone who had been a captain in the merchant marine or even a ship's master....Not surprisingly, discipline collapsed on French ships and insubordination became common.[20]

In other words, either extreme — aristocracy or democracy — had the same effect: a lack of hunger in the naval culture. Under aristocracy, common sailors were not motivated to excel because they could not rise to become an officer no matter what they did. Neither were they motivated under democracy; any meritocratic striving was stifled under the flawed doctrine of "equality." This fundamental difference in naval cultures naturally generated more hunger on the part of the British.

This cultural difference also created a mismatch in how French and British officers dealt with the chain of command and orders from the top. Not only was Villeneuve afraid of Nelson, but he was also afraid of Napoleon. Though Napoleon knew virtually nothing of sea warfare and Villeneuve was an experienced veteran, he never dared to challenge Napoleon's orders, even when he knew they were potentially disastrous. Nelson, on the other hand, was unburdened by any such dictatorial pressure or fear. British central command gave officers leeway and depended on their independent judgment, rather than dictating with force and fear from the top. Thus, Nelson was empowered to change battle tactics and make independent judgment calls, even when they violated protocol.

France's rigid aristocracy and then loose democracy created yet another problem: when top-notch officers were lost, they were extremely difficult, if not impossible, to replace. The British, on the other hand, had a large pool of hungry, qualified men to pull from. As Admiral Villeneuve wrote after the Battle of Trafalgar, "To any other nation, the loss of Nelson would have been irreparable; but in the British fleet...every captain was a Nelson."[21]

Britain's hungry naval culture also fostered innovation, while the French culture stifled it. In 1759, Admiral Edward Hawke innovated a new system of blockading at the Battle of Quiberon Bay, which we discussed in chapter three. His innovation allowed the Royal Navy to keep more than 14,000 men at sea for six months—an astronomical task. "The close blockade," Herman wrote, "had become a new strategic weapon in modern warfare and a hallmark of British naval dominance."[22]

The British never stopped improving. They continually trained and drilled and constantly strove to improve their tactics. One result of this ongoing improvement was that their experienced captains and well-trained crews were able to execute complex maneuvers nimbly in order to maintain high rates of fire from their cannons. As Michael A. Palmer wrote, "The ability of British men-of-war...to sustain rates of fire more than twice those of their French and Spanish opponents explains much of the Royal Navy's success."[23]

While the British were training and innovating, the French state of readiness was best described by Admiral Villeneuve, who lamented, "Our naval tactics are antiquated. We know nothing but how to place ourselves in line, and that is just what the enemy wants."[24]

Not only were French tactics antiquated, but they were also rigid—a product of the Enlightenment. Palmer explains:

Throughout the eighteenth century, European naval circles increasingly espoused the idea that scientific study could provide the answers to the difficult problems facing mariners and naval warriors....The French made a science of navies and naval warfare, complete with manuals and signal books meant to bring order to sailing-age battles formerly marked by disorder. And yet the French usually found themselves victimized by their far less scientific but far more successful British antagonists.[25]

The British method, in contrast, was best personified by Nelson. According to Palmer, his "decisionmaking process was not analytic but cybernetic. He did not so much weigh the pros and cons of any particular engagement as wade into the enemy with a firm conviction that the key to victory was simple: 'Lay a Frenchman close, and you will beat him.'"[26] The French method was aristocratic, scientific, logical, and rigid. The British method was meritocratic, aggressive, intuitive, and flexible, which was far more suited for the unpredictable chaos of naval battle. The British were guided by principles, to be sure, but were not entrenched in orthodoxy.

All of these cultural differences made for vast discrepancies in camaraderie (or lack thereof) aboard ship. The British *esprit de corps* was best expressed by Nelson when he wrote of his captains prior to the Battle of the Nile, quoting from Shakespeare's *Henry V*, "Such a gallant set of fellows! Such a band of brothers! My heart swells at the thought of them!"[27] Before engaging in the Battle of Trafalgar, one of Nelson's officers returned the compliment: "You are, my Lord, surrounded by friends whom you inspire with confidence."[28] While the British were inspired with confidence, the French captains, as one officer wrote, "…have no heart left to do well. Attention is not paid to signals….Discipline is utterly relaxed." Arthur Herman wrote that, "In contrast to Nelson's band of brothers, Villenueve was hardly on speaking terms with most of his officers."[29]

One final major cultural difference between the French and British should be noted. During the Napoleonic Wars, in which the French navy was routinely and soundly routed by the British, Napoleon's purpose was world domination. Animated primarily by Napoleon's indomitable will and power-crazed spirit, the French navy had no staying power. In short, its cause was not just. The British, in contrast, felt a duty to use their power for good, to balance global power and to defend their very homeland (always the staunchest of motivations). As Arthur Herman put it:

What democratic Athens had been [at the time of Alexander the Great], Great Britain was at the dawn of the Victorian age, the instrument for the "permanent improvement of mankind." Britain had a duty to make sure its sea power remained more dedicated to "the service of others, than of itself"—and that the Royal Navy continued to rule the waves.[30]

Understanding and Application

The French navy, though fairly evenly matched with the British in terms of size, technology, and firepower, could never achieve the dominance of the British. The difference was not technical, but cultural. The British were obsessive about winning; the French fought not to lose. The British were supremely confident; the French were often hesitant and doubtful. The British were hungry; the French were complacent. While the French culture was either aristocratic or democratic, depending on the season of history, the culture of the British navy was meritocratic. This made for rigidity and a lack of innovation on the part of the French but flexibility and innovation on the part of the British. The French, while fighting for conquest, were essentially mercenaries who enjoyed no camaraderie, while the British took great pride in fighting alongside their brothers in an idealistic duty to protect and serve the world.

Few examples offer such a stark reminder that all cultures are not equivalent. There are some cultural values and principles that generate success and others that spawn failure. This serves as a strong lesson to leaders that one of their most critical roles is to consciously cultivate culture. The French could have outspent the British. They could have amassed more ships, more firepower, and more technology. But without fundamental shifts in culture, none of those things would have made the difference. The British were stronger not in terms of iron, steel, timber, and canvas but rather in terms of resolve, confidence, and courage.

This example also illustrates how success breeds more success, and confidence begets more confidence. The British, driven by a moral and survival imperative, had no choice but to succeed. And as they did so, their confidence grew, and their success multiplied. The French, on the other hand, steadily declined in confidence and aggressiveness with each failure. Leaders first cultivate a culture of victory through unwavering principles. Then they build on each success to deepen the culture. They *never* accept failure. When they lose, they do not place blame or proffer excuses. They accept responsibility. They adjust, adapt, and innovate. Their pursuit of excellence is relentless, their resolve dauntless.

Summary

Tactics, strategy, and technical abilities are far less important than culture. Culture determines *how* strategies and tactics are determined and how they are executed. In a culture of performance, people are empowered to make independent judgment calls and decisions. Without being micromanaged, they take responsibility for the execution of ideas. They are not afraid to make mistakes; rather, their greater concern is with not taking action. They are held accountable for results, not how the results are achieved. They advance in rank based not on birth or privilege but on merit.

Values and traditions are the bedrock of culture, the DNA of your organization. Core values guide decisions. They are like an organization's conscience and help you realize when you've strayed. When an organization strays from its values without holding itself accountable, the culture will be eroded and distorted. Performance will plummet. Just as people intuitively feel when individuals are out of integrity, they also know when the organization they work in is out of integrity, out of alignment with its values.

A leader's primary role is to shape culture and hold the organization accountable to it. The leader is responsible for communicating to the team how critical the shared values are—not just through his or her words but, more importantly, through his or her actions. When people buy into the core values and see the leader living them, they are inspired to follow suit. They take pride in their shared identity. They strive to live up to the standards. Few things are harder to change in an organization than culture—and few things will give you greater leverage and influence.

CHAPTER NINE

The Lesson of the Unfair Load

Leadership Principle:

To accept the challenge of leadership is to accept responsibility. It is to shoulder burdens that others are unwilling to bear. It is to engage in a relentless pursuit of excellence, to never rest on your laurels, to always strive to improve your performance and results. A leader cannot blame anyone else for his or her team's lack of results. The only finger a leader can ever point — if he or she wants to be effective — is at him- or herself.

Many people aspire to leadership because of the potential glory it offers while being ignorant of the certain loneliness it requires. Before a leader can earn great rewards, he or she must first bear an unfair load. While a leader cannot point fingers of blame, there are always plenty of fingers pointed at a leader by other people. *Everyone* looks to the leader for ultimate responsibility. It's not fair; nor is it easy.

Illustration #1: Rodney at the Battle of the Saintes

In 1782, the final year of the American War of Independence, Sir George Rodney, while commanding a Royal Navy fleet, was discharged to the West Indies to shift the balance of naval power in the Caribbean. The British knew that the war in America was essentially over. But in the Caribbean, the French fleet commanded by Admiral comte de Grasse was still undefeated and powerful.

When Rodney reached the islands, he discovered that the French had already attacked Barbados (unsuccessfully) and captured St. Christopher. He was certain that next they would strike Jamaica, the crown jewel of Britain's Caribbean empire.

On April 8, the French fleet of thirty-five ships of the line left Martinique. Rodney set sail in pursuit with his thirty-seven ships and overtook the French fleet the next day. The British van began harassing the rear of the French fleet and heavily damaged one ship. They continued the pursuit over the next two days and overcame two stragglers. De Grasse turned his van around to protect the damaged ships. Rodney called off the engagement but continued following the fleet.

On the morning of April 12, the two fleets were just miles from the Dominica Passage between the northern end of Dominica and the Saintes. It's likely that de Grasse could have escaped through the channel—but not without leaving behind several damaged ships. Instead, he signaled for his fleet to form a line of battle. Rodney saw an opportunity to force a battle by passing his fleet across de Grasse's path. The two fleets engaged in parallel lines, sailing opposite of each other.

De Grasse was in a tight spot because he was running out of room to fight as he approached the passage. To stay engaged, at some point, he would have to turn his entire fleet around, exposing his line and making the fleet vulnerable to attack. When he signaled to the fleet to reverse course, his ships, under heavy fire, ignored the signal, and the French fleet continued on course to the south. He signaled two more times but to no avail. It wasn't until the wind changed that the ships were forced to alter their course, which put them directly under British fire. Gaps formed in the French formation, and Rodney led the way through one of them, with Admiral Hood leading the rear division through another. The day was lost for the French, their fleet shattered. The British captured five ships of the line that day, including de Grasse's flagship.

But there was to be more to the story that day. By breaking through the French line, Rodney had given the wind advantage to the French and inadvertently allowed their remaining ships to escape. As he put it, he "had not yet realized that the French ships were already slipping away to leeward through the great gaps in his own line, and round the southern end of it."[1] Rodney began pursuing the remaining French fleet but insisted that his fleet stay together, although many of his ships were heavily damaged and sailing poorly. That afternoon, they were able to run down and capture four ships of the line, including de Grasse's ship. This was the first time that the British had captured an enemy commander in chief.

Despite the coup, Rodney squandered a tremendous opportunity. By keeping his damaged fleet together, he had slowed down the pursuit and drastically limited the victory. Also, after capturing de Grasse, he stopped the pursuit entirely. As Hood wrote in a letter to Lord Sandwich:

My boat had scarcely boarded [de Grasse's flagship], but Sir George made the signal; and brought to, and continued to my utter astonishment to lay to the whole night. At this time 20 of the enemy's ships were within four miles of us, and some within two. In the morning not a ship of the flying enemy was to be seen, a misfortune that can never be sufficiently lamented.

In the glorious business of yesterday, I was most exceedingly disappointed in our Commander in chief. In the first instance that he did not make the signal for a general chase the instant he hauled *that* down for the line of battle; had he done so, I am confident we should have had full twenty sail of the enemy's line of battle ships in possession before dark.[2]

Hood was not the only frustrated subordinate of Rodney. Captain William Cornwallis, who had commanded

Rodney's center division, wrote a poem to commemorate the battle, wherein he wrote: "Had a chief worthy Britain commanded our fleet, twenty-five good French ships had been laid at our feet."[3]

The next day, Hood raised the issue with Rodney. Rodney's reply was essentially a shoulder shrug: "Come, we have done very handsomely as it is."[4]

Understanding and Application

Rodney's skill and valor won a British victory. Yet his contentment with what he gained caused him to ignore what he *could have* gained. Had he been hungrier, his victory could have been significantly greater, and he could have struck a devastating blow to the French.

Even in victory, leaders are held accountable to a high standard. For true leaders, good enough is never good enough. Leaders never stop striving to win—even and especially after they have won. After they achieve one level, they set their sights on the next level. Slacking off is a luxury afforded only to people who don't want to carry the burden of leadership.

Illustration #2: Byng at the Battle of Minorca

The opening sea battle of the Seven Years' War between Great Britain and France was fought for control of the island of Minorca, to the east of Spain and south of France. On April 1, 1756, Vice-Admiral John Byng was commissioned by the Admiralty to lead a fleet to the Mediterranean. His instructions were "drafted in a general fashion to meet a variety of contingencies, and heavily reliant on the commander's good sense and willingness to shoulder responsibility," as Michael A. Palmer wrote.[5]

He was directed to sail to Gibraltar and there determine his next course of action. If the Toulon squadron had passed the strait, he would send reinforcements to Canada. If not, his course would be to protect the British garrison at Minorca. As his instructions put it, in that case, he was to: "go on without a moment's loss of time to Minorca, and if you find any attack made on that island by the French, you are to use all possible means in your power for its relief."[6]

When Byng set sail from England to the Mediterranean on April 6, he was unhappy with his command. He complained to one of his captains, Augustus Hervey, that Lord Anson of the Admiralty had reserved the best ships for Hawke, who was commanding the Western Squadron, and had dispatched the worst ships to the Mediterranean. Byng's complaints were seemingly justifiable; he had been given no storeships, fireships, hospital ships, or tenders, and his fleet was undermanned. But as Palmer wrote:

> ...however justified Byng's disgust with the state of his fleet, his willingness to share his views with his subordinates could not but undermine their confidence. How well were officers and men who were told that theirs were the worst ships in the navy likely to respond in battle? Moreover, while Byng did not publicly voice doubts about the quality of his captains, they must have surmised that in their commander's mind, if Anson had not sent the best

ships out with Byng, he probably had not sent the best officers either.[7]

When he reached Gibraltar on May 2, Byng learned that the French had already landed on Minorca and had attacked the British garrison with 14,000 men. His mission was clear: protect Minorca. But Lieutenant General Thomas Fowke, who was commanding the garrison at Gibraltar, felt that Minorca could not be saved and that it would be futile to send his troops to help. He expressed his opinion to Byng in a council of war, and Byng agreed with him. He didn't set sail for Minorca until May 8, and when he did, he sailed with the belief that it was a lost cause.

The truth is, as historians have concluded, that it was far from a lost cause. The French were suffering from disease, were short on supplies, and were far weaker than Byng realized. Byng's primary objective was to establish a naval presence to lift the siege. Accomplishing this didn't require that he destroy the strong French naval squadron established there; preventing the transport of supplies would have worked nicely.

Byng reached Minorca on May 19. The French fleet arrived the next morning, and Byng prepared his ships for battle. During the battle, several opportunities arose for Byng to take advantage of the French. But doing so would have required him to break the line ahead formation, which he was hesitant to do considering that the Admiralty had court-martialed other officers for doing so. But his hesitancy and unwillingness to "shoulder responsibility" and take initiative lost the battle.

For several days after the battle, Byng anchored off Minorca and repaired his fleet, making no attempt to aid or even communicate with the garrison on the island. On May 24, he convened a council of war and convinced his officers that they could do nothing to help the garrison. They promptly left Minorca and sailed to Gibraltar, leaving the sieged garrison with no hope of relief.

News of Byng's failure to relieve Minorca reached London in mid-July. He was hauled in for a court-martial and found guilty of failing to "do his utmost" to prevent Minorca from falling to the French. He was sentenced to death and shot by a firing squad on May 14, 1757. (Apparently, the English read Voltaire and heeded his sarcastic advice that "in this country it is found good, from time to time, to kill one Admiral to encourage the others."[8])

Understanding and Application

Byng's ultimate failure was not tactical or strategic; it was the fact that, from the beginning, he failed to accept the unfair load of leadership. Had he chosen to do so, there was significant opportunity for the battle to have turned out differently. A blockade could have prevented French troops from receiving badly needed supplies. The French fleet could have been beaten. Troops could have been conveyed from Gibraltar to aid the sieged troops on Minorca. Byng could have stayed to help the troops. He could have decided that come hell or high water, he was going to remain at his post and do his duty. But his circumstances weren't fair, and he didn't want to accept them.

To put it bluntly, sometimes leadership stinks. Sometimes you're placed in a position where you have a severe disadvantage. Sometimes you're lacking in resources, people, and skills. Sometimes you're called to enter what appears to be a losing battle. You have two choices: you can shirk, or you can deal with it.

Illustration #3: The "Sea Wolf" at the Battle of Basque Roads

One of the most colorful characters of the age of fighting sail was Scottish captain Thomas Cochrane. A mercenary with a fiery temperament and later a radical politician, what Cochrane lacked in diplomacy he made up for with an abundance of courage, tenacity, and creativity. In chapter three, we highlighted his astounding story of capturing the Spanish frigate *El Gamo*, although being outnumbered six to one.

Cochrane's specialty was sailing with a handful of small vessels, rather than a large fleet of line-of-battle ships, and harassing the enemy with speedy attacks and nimble maneuvers. He was particularly skilled in coastal warfare, using unpredictable strategies and meticulously planning each operation. During his thirteen-month cruise as commander of the little *Speedy*, Cochrane captured, burned, or drove ashore fifty-three ships before being captured by the French in July 1801. (He was held only a few days before being traded for a French officer.) His exploits led the

French to nickname him *Le Loup des Mers* (the Sea Wolf). One of his peers, Vice-Admiral Cuthbert Collingwood, praised him in letters to the Admiralty, writing:

> Nothing can exceed the activity and zeal with which his lordship pursues the enemy. The success which attends his enterprises clearly indicates with what skill and ability they are conducted; besides keeping the coast [of France] in constant alarm, causing a total suspension of trade, and harassing a body of troops employed in opposing him, he has, probably, prevented those troops…from advancing into Spain, by giving them employment in the defence of their own coasts.[9]

In February 1809, a French fleet led by Rear-Admiral Willaumez had taken shelter in a safe anchorage known as Basque Roads, on the Bay of Biscay on the western coast of France. The anchorage was protected from the weather as well as from enemy attack by virtue of several islands, which made navigation in the area difficult and slow. The area was also extremely difficult to blockade. Admiral James Gambier was sent with a fleet to blockade the anchorage. But the Admiralty, knowing how easily the French could escape from the area, wanted action. They proposed an attack using fireships, small vessels loaded with explosives that were set on fire and steered into enemy ships. Gambier was reluctant to try the idea and replied to the Admiralty that "an attack by means of fireships was hazardous, if not desperate…[but] if the Board of Admiralty wished to order such an attack, it should be done secretly and quickly."[10]

This, the Admiralty knew, was a job for the cagey Cochrane. Although only a junior captain, Cochrane was sent to assist Gambier, which caused Gambier to fly into a rage. But he had no choice but to accept Cochrane. Cochrane immediately jumped into action and prepared vessels full of shells and rockets. On the evening of April 11, Cochrane, who always led from the front, joined the crew of the boat that was to set fire to the first fireship. They got as close to the enemy as possible, lit the fuses, and beat a hasty retreat. Heavy winds caused the fuses to burn much faster than they were supposed to. Cochrane explained:

> To our consternation, the fuses which had been constructed to burn fifteen minutes, lasted little more than half that time, when the vessel blew up, filling the air with shells, grenades, and rockets; whilst the downward and lateral force of the explosion raised a solitary mountain of water, from the breaking of which in all directions our little boat narrowly escaped being swamped. In one respect it was, perhaps, fortunate for us that the fuses did not burn the time calculated, as, from the little way we had made against the strong head wind and tied, the rockets and shells from the exploded vessel went over us. Had we been in the line of their descent, at the moment of explosion, our destruction, from the

shower of broken shells and other missiles, would have been inevitable.[11]

Despite feeling relieved that they had escaped the blast, Cochrane was disappointed to see that only four of their twenty-one fireships actually reached the enemy. The attack still worked, however: The French panicked and cut their anchor cables to drift away from the danger. By daylight, though not one French battleship had burned, eight of them had run aground and only two were still afloat.

Cochrane, seeing the stranded ships, was eager to finish the battle. It would be a simple matter to sail into the harbor and bombard the grounded French ships before they could get loose. He anxiously signaled for support to Gambier, who was anchored ten miles away. A few hours later, Gambier moved his ships closer, but fearing that he would run aground himself, he anchored six miles away. One sailor noted that "this would have been the time to have destroyed them; but this favourable opportunity was neglected, which caused not a little murmuring against us, and was considered most unseamanlike by many experienced men in our fleet."[12]

By midday, some of the French ships began to refloat. Cochrane, furious at the lost opportunity, decided not to wait for Gambier. He sailed for the French himself in his small vessel while urgently signaling for Gambier to follow. Gambier reluctantly sent in a handful of smaller vessels. By late afternoon, the British had captured three ships, with Cochrane capturing the fifty-gun *Calcutta* with his thirty-eight-gun *Imperieuse*.

The battle was hailed a victory for the British, but Cochrane was disappointed that it was not nearly as complete as it could have been. Interestingly, Napoleon agreed with Cochrane. A physician by the name of O'Meara published a conversation he had with Napoleon on St. Helena, wherein he said:

> I [O'Meara] said that it was the opinion of a very distinguished naval officer whom I named, and who was well known to him, that if Cochrane had been properly supported, he would have destroyed the whole of the French ships. "He could not only have destroyed them," replied Napoleon, "but he might and would have taken them out [captured them], had your admiral supported him as he ought to have done....The terror of the *brûlots* (fire-ships) was so great that they actually threw their powder overboard, so that they could have offered very little resistance. The French admiral was an *imbecille*, but yours was just as bad. I assure you, that if Cochrane had been supported, he would have taken every one of the ships."[13]

This story is interesting in and of itself. But what makes it even more interesting is the fact that Cochrane was serving as a junior captain under Gambier. After his capture of the *Gamo* eight years earlier, by all rights, he should have received a promotion. Cochrane had fought a long political battle with the Admiralty for a promotion, not only for himself but for his officers as well. The Admiralty refused his petitions.

Understanding and Application

Lesser men, after being scorned by the Admiralty, as was Cochrane after capturing the *Gamo*, would have been offended and bitterly resigned their posts. But eight years after being snubbed, Cochrane was still in the trenches, serving under inferior captains. He had moved on from the unfairness and had resolved to continue doing what he could with what he had where he was.

Life isn't always fair. Qualified leaders are often overlooked and ignored. The mark of a leader is what he does after such an experience. True leaders do the right thing regardless of circumstances, regardless of being mistreated. They are driven not by external recognition but by internal integrity.

Illustration #4: Cochrane Capturing the *Esmeralda*

In late 1818, after a stock exchange scandal, Thomas Cochrane left England and sailed to Chile, where he took command of Chile's navy in its war for independence against Spain. By 1820, the Spanish had but one stronghold left in Callao and Lima, on the midwestern coast of Peru. Preparations were made for a decisive battle. General José de San Martín was in charge of the land forces, with Cochrane in charge of the navy responsible for giving San Martín's troops support from sea.

218

On August 21, 1820, the squadron with 4,200 troops left Valparaíso for Callao. Cochrane was under the belief that they would sail directly to Callao and instigate a battle without delay. But San Martín, a "cautious" general to put it nicely (Cochrane viewed his caution as cowardice), decided to land at Truxillo, which was hundreds of miles away from the Spanish troops. Cochrane was confused and frustrated; he wanted the land troops to land close to the enemy targets so that he could aid the attack by sea. He saw no point in landing at Truxillo, where "the army could have gained no advantage, nor, indeed, have found anything to do, except to remain there safe from any attack by the Spaniards."[14]

San Martín soon revised his plan and had Cochrane's fleet convey his troops to Pisco, which was closer to Callao but still 150 miles away. There he remained for seven weeks, which infuriated Cochrane. Even while at Pisco, which was defended by only 300 Spanish troops, San Martín never attacked the Spanish. On October 28, San Martín finally agreed to continue to Callao. But when they reached Callao, he vacillated yet again and insisted that he and his troops be taken back to Ancón, thirty miles to the south.

Cochrane had reached the limits of his patience. Though he had no control over San Martín's plans and could not disobey his commands, he could still act on his own initiative. He left San Martín's troops at Ancón and then sailed back to Callao with three ships, telling San Martín that he was going to blockade the port so that Lima could not be reinforced by sea. But a blockade was but a small part of his intentions, though he did not confide his plan to San Martín.

While at Callao, he used the fifty-gun flagship, the *O'Higgins*, for reconnaissance to gauge the Spanish forces. Callao, he discovered, was heavily defended by shore batteries and the forty-four-gun *Esmeralda*, the most powerful Spanish warship on the coast. If he could destroy *Esmeralda*, the garrison would be significantly weakened. But Cochrane had something different in mind: boarding and capturing the ship. Always unpredictable, he knew that no one would ever expect him to be foolish enough to try it. The ship was securely anchored and protected by 300 pieces of artillery on land and twenty-seven gunboats and several armed block-ships. This wouldn't be the first time that Cochrane had been underestimated.

On the afternoon of November 5, Cochrane announced to his crews that he was about to strike "a mortal blow" to the Spanish and promised them, "The value of all the vessels captured in Callao will be yours."[15] Of the hundreds of volunteers who stepped forward, he chose 160 seamen and eighty marines and prepared to attack that night. As evening descended, he anchored his fleet ships far enough out to sea to put the Spanish off their guard. Then, the men, each armed with a pistol and cutlass for hand-to-hand fighting, boarded fourteen small boats, with Cochrane in the lead boat.

After two hours of rowing to the *Esmeralda*, the attack itself lasted no more than fifteen minutes. Cochrane led one division to one side of the ship, while another division rowed to the other side. Cochrane was the first to climb up the main-chains. When he poked his head above deck, he was struck in the head by a sentry's musket butt. He fell and landed on the pin on which the oar of his boat rested, which drove into his back near the spine. He ignored the pain and climbed again, this time with pistol in hand. When he reached the top, he shot the sentry and then shouted to his men, "Up, my lads! She's ours!"[16]

The Spanish had been sleeping on their guns. They arose quickly and defended the ship as Cochrane's men swarmed up and over the sides. The Spanish withdrew to the forecastle and began sweeping the deck with musket fire. One shot hit Cochrane in the thigh. He bound his leg with a handkerchief and limped to the quarterdeck, where he stood on one leg, laying the injured leg on hammock netting, and continued directing the attack. After a fierce fight, the Spanish commander surrendered. Cochrane had lost only eleven men, and just thirty had been wounded.

Prior to the attack, Cochrane, always the meticulous planner, had ordered several men to prepare *Esmeralda's* rigging for sail as soon as they boarded the ship. Immediately after the Spanish surrendered, Cochrane set sail in the captured ship for the open sea. The danger now was heavy fire from shore. But Cochrane had prepared for this as well. In the harbor were an American ship, the *Macedonian*, and a British ship, the *Hyperion*. America and Britain were neutrals in the fight, and Cochran knew that the Spanish would not risk sinking one of their ships. So he ordered that the *Esmeralda* hoist lights identical to those found on the American and British ships. Immediately, the guns on shore ceased, and the *Esmeralda* continued sailing unmolested.

Cochrane had planned to use the *Esmeralda* to attack and cut adrift every other anchored Spanish ship. But after he was wounded, another commander took charge and, despite Cochrane's protests, simply sailed the ship out to sea. Even still, it was a major coup. It crippled the Spanish defenses and opened the way to their eventual defeat.

Understanding and Application

Upon realizing that San Martín had no intention of directly attacking the Spanish at Callao, Cochrane could have thrown up his hands and sat idle, awaiting further commands. San Martín was, after all, in charge. But to Cochrane, this was unthinkable. He wouldn't be insubordinate, but he didn't have to sit around. He took the initiative and acted within his realm of authority and influence to strike a crushing blow to the enemy.

Far too often, people sit around and await instructions from top leaders. But leadership can be initiated at any level of any organization. You don't need permission or commands to make a difference. This doesn't mean that you should overstep the boundaries of your authorities or disregard rules. But it does mean that you can be creative and innovative and do everything you can within your sphere of influence.

Illustration #5: Nelson's Bravery and Battle Wounds

We've spoken much of Horatio Nelson's exploits—and indeed, his life was worthy of being studied. In addition to his specific battles, much can be learned from his general demeanor in battle. Nelson was always a leader from the front. He was always in the thick of things.

During an attack at Corsica in 1794, his forces landed and began moving guns ashore and positioning them in the heights surrounding the town. As usual, Nelson was stationed at the front. One of the enemy shots struck a sandbag protecting his position and sprayed stones and sand. He was struck by debris in his right eye. He quickly had the wound bandaged and returned to action. He lost the sight of that eye. In 1797, he lost his right arm in the Battle of Santa Cruz de Tenerife when he was hit by grape-shot. As usual, he was leading the charge.

During the Battle of the Nile in Aboukir Bay in 1798, he was hit in the forehead by a shot fragment and badly wounded. He was carried below deck for treatment. Medics of the time did not use triage procedures to determine which wounded soldier to treat first. Instead, they treated one soldier at a time as they were brought to them. Of course, special treatment was afforded for officers. But Nelson refused to be treated ahead of his wounded sailors in line before him. "No," he said, when he was offered to be treated immediately, "I will take my turn with my brave fellows."[17]

During the fierce battle at Copenhagen in 1801, with cannonballs "howling and snapping" over his head, he turned to his aide and said with a smile, "It is warm work, and this day may be the last to us at any moment…but mark you, I would not be elsewhere for thousands."[18] Michael A. Palmer writes that during his most famous battle at Trafalgar, Nelson:

> …remained on the quarterdeck throughout the battle, in full dress, highly visible and highly vulnerable. As men dropped around him, he remained, pacing and unperturbed. A French cannonball hit the deck and bounced howling between him and his flag captain, Thomas Hardy. He again smiled and said "This is too warm work, Hardy, to last long."[19]

Soon after, he was mortally wounded by a sharpshooter.

Understanding and Application

Accepting the unfair load of leadership means that you don't baby yourself. You don't expect special treatment by virtue of your title or position. You don't stay aloof from the muck and the blood, the chaos and confusion of battle. A true leader accepts more responsibility and works harder than everyone else. A true leader doesn't focus on the privileges he or she can garner but rather on the service he or she can render.

Summary

US President Harry Truman kept a sign on his desk that expressed the lesson of the unfair load well. It said: "The buck stops here."[20] Effective leadership is an exercise in extreme responsibility. Even when other people are to blame for something that goes wrong, you can't point fingers at anyone except yourself. A true leader never whines that his or her people "just don't get it." Rather, a true leader asks him- or herself, "Where have *I* failed? What must *I* learn from this? What more can *I* do?" Great leaders are hard on themselves and easy on others. That example of extreme personal accountability inspires others to follow suit and creates a culture of accountability.

As a leader, you *will* be required to deal with things that are unfair. You will be called to shoulder extra burdens. People will blame you for things that really aren't your fault. You will be criticized and scorned, overlooked and belittled, neglected and rejected. But if you stick with it through those hard times, you will also be recognized, praised, and rewarded. You will grow in ability and influence. You will feel the profound satisfaction that only comes from knowing you have made a difference.

There's nothing easy about leadership. But those willing to accept the unfair load "wouldn't be elsewhere for thousands," as Lord Nelson put it.

CHAPTER TEN

The Lesson of the Fog of Battle

Leadership Principle:

Leaders must deal in reality, and often that reality is complex and ever-changing. Complexity, however, is no excuse for lack of results. Leaders, despite their circumstances, the pressures they face, the long odds they confront, and the machinations against them, are still, in the end, held accountable for results. If there were a Leadership Hall of Fame (as I think there should be), there would certainly be no section dedicated to the "Yeah, buts."

Leaders will *never* find clarity by looking outside themselves. Were external circumstances clear and simple, leadership would not be needed. The whole point of leadership is that you're called to successfully navigate the battlefield — with all its smoke and mud, blood and gore. Screaming shells are raining down on your crew. Your perfectly devised plan has collapsed. Chaos reigns. It is precisely your job as a leader to make sense of the chaos and chart a path to victory.

The only clarity to be found in this process is by looking inside yourself, finding and trusting your intuition, and holding on tightly to your purpose and vision. You can't clear the fog of battle, but you can clear your mental fog and take action.

Illustration #1: The Illusory Allure of Communications

Writing of the "crucial paradox of knowledge," author Jacob Bronowski said:

> Year by year we devise more precise instruments with which to observe nature. And when we look at the observations, we are discomfited to see that they are still fuzzy, and we feel that they are as uncertain as ever. We seem to be running after a goal that lurches away from us to infinity every time we come within sight of it.[1]

Communications in naval warfare provide a perfect example of this. In Nelson's day, commanders believed that flag signals could solve their problems of command and control. In our day, naval officers believe radio, telecommunications, or digital technologies can solve the same problems Nelson faced. But the problems remain the same. It's tempting to believe that improved communications can clear the fog of battle. And indeed, it certainly can help leaders to make better, more informed decisions. But no matter how well officers and troops can communicate with each other, no matter how accurate a leader's data and intelligence, the fog of battle is an inevitable reality.

One primary reason, Michael A. Palmer explains, is because as communication technology advances, it changes the nature of warfare itself, often to the detriment of commanders. For example, when Nelson approached Trafalgar with his fleet, his sailors had time to eat dinner because the approach took hours. But today, commanders often have only seconds to make crucial decisions. Today's commanders, using technology far in advance of what was available to Nelson and Cochrane, receive more data, but the increased complexity in modern warfare has outpaced the improvements in communications technology.[2]

We'd like to think that uncertainty is simply caused by not having all of the information—that if we could simply gather all the information, uncertainty would be eliminated. But like the pot of gold at the end of the rainbow, this is a delusion; the closer we feel we are approaching to certainty, the more it eludes us. Nothing is more certain in battle than uncertainty, which J.D. Steinbruner defines as "imperfect correspondence between information and environment."[3] As Michael A. Palmer wrote:

There exists an evident tendency in some contemporary naval circles to view communications and information technology as the answer to the problems of command and the means by which the fog of war can be dissipated....But the same expectations were held of flag signals late in the eighteenth century and of the radio in the years between the world wars.

Nelson understood that the fog of war was not a cloud of uncertainty that could be whisked away if only the appropriate communicative means were at hand, but an element inherent to warfare as to life itself: an element as resistant to the dissipatory effects of commanders as real fog was to the blows of a sword. That element, like fog, could protectively enshroud a force led by men prepared to make decisions on their own within a tactical framework provided by their superior.[4]

Illustration #2: The General Complexities of Wooden-Ship Warfare

Forget the fog of battle. Simply sailing a ship in the age of fighting sail presented a staggering level of complexity for commanders to deal with. The fog of battle simply added more chaos and confusion to the existing complexity. Speaking of large ships of the line, Barbara Tuchman wrote:

With its motor power dependent on the caprice of heaven and direction-finding on the distant stars, and its central piece of equipment—the mast—dependent on seasoned timber that was rarely obtainable, and control of locomotion dependent on rigging and ropes of a complexity to defy philosophers of the Sorbonne, much less the homeless untutored poor off the streets who made up the crews, and communication from commander to his squadron dependent on signal flags easily obscured by distance or smoke from the guns or by pitching of the ship, these cumbersome vehicles were as convenient as if dinosaurs had survived to be used by cowboys for driving cattle.[5]

It's a wonder that naval commanders were able to keep their cool and direct all the moving parts of a ship in peacetime, let alone during battle. In truth, to be effective, captains could not do everything alone; they had to rely on their men for execution, both for sailing and for fighting.

Understanding and Application

The first step in dealing with the fog of battle is to simply accept it as an inherent reality—not as something that can be cleared away with improved intelligence, but as something that can *never* be cleared and must simply be dealt with. Leaders must learn to tolerate a certain level of chaos. They can't sit around waiting for the clouds to clear. They have to gather as much information as they can and then choose and act as best as they can.

Leaders can devise the perfect plan on paper. But once they enter the battlefield, they encounter what the brilliant military theorist Carl von Clausewitz termed "friction," meaning the "factors that distinguish real war from war on paper."[6] Even if you have clarity before the battle, eventually the fog will rise, and circumstances will change. The plan will have to be adapted — and quickly.

Nothing gives a leader the ability to adapt quickly to the fog of battle than empowering his or her people to act independently and innovatively. Decentralization, then, becomes not just a temporary strategy but a permanent imperative for dealing with chaos and complexity. A style of centralized command and control cripples teams and organizations when the fog rises. Every individual in battle sees a different perspective than everyone else. Your people on the ground, in the trenches, see things that you can't see. Sometimes you don't have the luxury of instantaneous communication to make immediate adjustments from the top; many times, those adjustments have to come from other people than the leader.

If you've empowered your people and developed them as courageous and innovative leaders, you can trust their decisions in the fog. You can send them into the thick of battle with confidence that they can make effective adjustments without you making specific orders for every contingency.

Illustration #3: Nelson's Quick Decisions at the Battle of Cape St. Vincent

You'll recall that in chapter three, we highlighted the Battle of Cape St. Vincent, wherein Lord Nelson boarded and captured two Spanish ships: the *San Nicolas* and then the *San Josef* from the deck of the *San Nicolas*. The incredibly bold move was dubbed "Nelson's patent bridge for boarding first rates." The battle illustrated Nelson's ability and willingness to take initiative. But it also illustrated something more: his ability to make quick and effective decisions in the fog of battle.

Nelson's ship, the *Captain*, was in the rear of the British fleet, where he had an excellent view of the battle. He was alarmed when he watched one of the Spanish columns turning in order to get around the British ships in the rear. If he were to follow orders and continue in the line, the Spanish could pose a serious threat. He ignored orders and broke rank to turn out of the line and cut off the Spanish. This decision was not without risk; had his action failed, he would have been court-martialed for disobeying orders. Furthermore, it placed his ship in a position where it would be subjected to heavy fire from seven Spanish ships. Arthur Herman wrote:

To the astonished Spaniards, it must have seemed suicide. His fellow officers watching from the other ships had to agree; if the Spanish did not kill him, then Jervis surely would for disobeying his order. But Nelson had carefully calculated his odds. He knew is crewmen were the best trained and motivated fighting seamen in the world, while many of the Spanish were landlubber conscripts and their officers sloppy and inexperienced. Each of his gun crews could swab, load, run out, and fire two broad-sides every three minutes. The Spanish would be lucky to get off one broadside in five.[7]

The move took the Spanish by surprise and turned them away, like "turning them as two shepherd's dogs wou'd a flock of sheep,"[8] as one sailor later described.

That was Nelson's first critical decision. His next came when his ship had been shot to pieces and rendered useless. Rather than simply trying to drift away, Nelson worked with what he had in that moment and chose to engage. He moved his boat into position to board the *San Nicolas* and captured it within a few moments.

His final split-second decision in the fog of battle came when sailors from the *San Josef* began firing on the British sailors aboard the *San Nicolas*. Again, Nelson could have retreated. But instead, he instantly called for his men to board and capture the *San Josef* from the deck of the *San Nicolas*. Never before had this been seen in naval warfare. It was as shocking as it was unprecedented.

Understanding and Application

At several times throughout the battle, Nelson made snap decisions, all of which could have either ended his naval career or his life. He didn't have all of the information, and he had very little time. He made the decisions anyway, and they made all the difference to the outcome of the Battle of Cape St. Vincent.

As a leader, you will often be forced to make quick decisions. You won't have as much information or as much time as you would like. But a decision must be made anyway. In these moments, what will matter most is your previous preparation. Preparation helps you to master the basics and develop "unconscious competence," where you do things automatically without having to think about them. The more things you master and the greater your unconscious competence, the easier and better your decisions in the heat of the moment. Nelson's decisions at the Battle of Cape St. Vincent weren't simply impetuous and hasty—the products of a young and naïve mind. Though quick and bold, they were the careful calculations made from almost three decades of experience. We laud Nelson's split-second decisions in the heat of battle, but never forget that those decisions were the result of his tireless preparation long beforehand.

When decisions must be made under fire, the first thing you must do is prioritize. Determine what the most important considerations are in that precise moment. Understand that risks will have to be taken, and casualties will undoubtedly be suffered. But what must you make happen, no matter what? What must be protected at all costs? What must be accomplished right now to enable long-term success?

Once you've properly prioritized, the next step is to focus. Eliminate the distractions, cancel out the chaos, reduce the complexity to the most critical elements through laser focus. When Nelson's ship was disabled, he didn't throw his hands up in despair. He didn't try to drift away from the battle. He didn't squander his energy and resources by trifling with petty details. He sized up the situation and chose the path that would inflict the most damage on the enemy in that moment. His decision to board the enemy ship made every one of his challenges obsolete. It kept him engaged and caused the tipping point of the battle. This is the result of effective prioritization and crystal-clear focus.

Summary

The fog of battle is an inescapable reality. No amount of technology or communications can ever eliminate it. Leadership in any field or endeavor is an exercise in wading through complexity. A leader's job is to make sense of that complexity and successfully plan and fight through it to achieve results. A leader cannot make excuses. Yes, navigating through the fog is incredibly difficult. Yes, the risks are very high, the consequences very real. Were it not so, leadership would not be required—and nothing worthwhile would stand to be gained.

So how best to battle difficult circumstances and unfair pressures? The key is to keep things simple. Focus on priorities. The easiest way to do this is to go all the way to the "30,000-foot view" and remember your overall purpose. What got you into this position of responsibility in the first place? At one point, I would hope, you were convinced that what you were doing was worthwhile. What was the basis for that decision? Why did it matter so much to you? More succinctly, what was the vision you had of what could be? What part of the status quo did you absolutely deplore?

You see, leaders are such because they find something they cannot stand to leave the way they found it. Some situation seemed wrong to them or perhaps not as right as it could be. Somebody was hurting or suffering and needed a leader to step in. Someone was being wronged and needed defending. Some rule was unfair. Some government was unlawful. Some project was unfinished. These are the roots of leadership because they speak directly to a leader's discontentment.

When a person of character is confronted with such a situation, that person becomes a leader because he or she cannot stand to leave the situation the way he or she found it. A vision of how things could be better forms in the leader's mind, and he or she can't let go of it, nor it of the leader. This vision of how things could be improved causes a hunger inside the leader for change. The tension the leader feels when considering his or her vision is priceless because it's the driving force behind leadership. A leader confronted with unfair circumstances and overwhelming pressures must first go back to the vision and his or her overriding purpose in life. From there, everything will look a little clearer.

The next thing to do is prioritize amid the fog. Find out the one or two *best* things to do, and get started on them right away. Remember, there are a lot of *good* things to do but usually only one or two *best* things to do. Focus on those, and temporarily disregard the rest. As the Bible says in Matthew 6:34 (KJV), "Sufficient unto the day is the evil thereof."

After remembering his or her purpose and focusing on priorities, the leader must next find someone to serve. When things get tough, when the way seems unclear, finding someone to help, love, and serve is the biggest pressure reliever known to man.

Above all, never, ever give up. Don't quit the job before it is done. Finish when you finish. Whether it takes you three months or three years, finish what you started out to do. This may take adapting to realities and changing your strategies. You may have to go around when you thought you could go through. You may lose your progress and have to start over. You may, like Nelson, find yourself in a ship that won't sail and have very few options. Remember why you started fighting in the first place. Prioritize. Focus. Find a way.

A leader who implements these basics during the fog of battle will be surprised at his or her results, and results, after all, are what a leader is held accountable for.

CHAPTER ELEVEN

The Lesson of Legacy

Leadership Principle:

All human beings hope that they will be missed after their death. But true leaders don't just want to be missed; they want their legacy to continue. If you've done a poor job as a leader, you may be missed upon your death, but your vision, purpose, dreams, and value will not be perpetuated. They will die with you. If you've done a great job as a leader, other leaders whom you have developed will step up to take your place.

The best leaders leave a legacy in the lives of other leaders. They build not an army of sycophantic, blind followers but an army of independent, empowered leaders. The true legacy of a great leader is not what he or she accomplishes in his or her lifetime; it's what the leaders he or she has developed continue building long after he or she is gone. It is not measured by the stone the leader drops in the water alone but also by the ripples he or she causes.

Illustration #1: The Royal Navy after Nelson's Death

You'll recall from chapter eight that the French Admiral Villenueve wrote after Nelson's death at Trafalgar, "To any other nation, the loss of Nelson would have been irreparable; but in the British fleet...every captain was a Nelson."[1] His words proved to be prophetic.

As overwhelming as Britain's victory was at Trafalgar, Napoleon was still the dominant force in Europe. Nelson won the battle at Trafalgar, but the war was still very much in question. Sixteen French and Spanish ships had escaped the battle and were ready to fight again. France had another thirteen ships of the line at Brest and also rebuilt its fleet feverishly. The Royal Navy still faced a tremendous challenge that would tax its resources, skill, and ingenuity to the fullest. Indeed, the Napoleonic Wars would continue for another ten years after Trafalgar. But as Arthur Herman wrote:

> Fortunately, the British navy soon discovered, somewhat to its own surprise, it could do without Nelson. After the Age of Nelson, there followed what could almost be called the Age of Nelsons, as a series of bold and brilliant naval commanders stepped forward and won the war he had left unfinished.
>
> They began with Nelson's own band of brothers....Taken together, the band of brothers formed a living legacy for the British navy. Direct descendants of five...would be naval officers on the eve of World War I.[2]

After Nelson's death, Napoleon hoped that his navy could finally gain the advantage over the British. But defeat after defeat suffered at the hands of the leader-saturated Royal Navy convinced him that they could not be defeated by conventional naval strategies. Herman continued, "Theoretically, at least, the fleets of France and its allies should have outnumbered the British fleet by 160 battleships to 110. Practically, however, they were too scattered, and too hemmed in by the British blockade, to ever combine into an effective force."[3] Napoleon gave up the fight on sea and decided instead to "conquer the sea by land," meaning to choke off Britain's trade.

But the British proved to be far superior in this enterprise as well. Between 1793 and 1815, the French navy and privateers captured more than 11,000 British merchant ships, which only represented 2.5 percent of Britain's total shipping. The British merchant fleet continued to grow during that period despite the French threat. In contrast, the British navy's blockade effectively shut down the trade of every nation facing the Mediterranean, Atlantic, or Baltic.

Napoleon dominated on land but never could break the stronghold of the Royal Navy, the strength of which was, in large part, the direct result of Nelson's legacy.

Understanding and Application

Had Nelson been merely a superstar admiral, his impact and legacy would have died with him. Genuine leadership is about far more than personal performance. It's even about more than immediate results. It's about long-term, generational impact and results. It's about developing other leaders who can continue your personal ripple effect and build it into waves.

In *Launching a Leadership Revolution*, which I coauthored with Orrin Woodward, we detail the five levels of leadership and explain the important difference between merely developing followers and developing other leaders:

1. Learning
2. Performing
3. Leading
4. Developing Leaders
5. Developing Leaders Who Develop Leaders...

At Level 4, leaders are not just developing followers; they are developing leaders. There is a big difference between the two.

Empowering leaders involves giving them control and decision-making authority. It means letting them lead their own teams and make their own mistakes and, quite simply, giving them the freedom to fail or fly. True leaders will not stick with the Level 4 Leader unless given a chance to spread their wings and show what they can do because without that chance, they will never reach their potential. This is why it is said that average leaders lead followers, while great leaders lead leaders.[4]

Nelson began learning naval warfare at the age of twelve. He learned how to perform and lead. But fortunately for the Royal Navy, he didn't stop there. He encouraged his people to spread their wings. He empowered them to exercise initiative. He allowed them to try and fail. In short, he developed other leaders. As Nathan Miller wrote, speaking of Nelson's pursuit of the French preceding the Battle of the Nile:

> Throughout the voyage, whenever the weather permitted, he invited groups of his captains to *Vanguard's* great cabin, where, over dinner, as Captain Berry related, "he would fully develop to them his own ideas of the different and best modes of attack, and such plans as he proposed to execute upon falling in with the Enemy, whatever their position might be, by day or night." In this "school for captains" they came to know Nelson's intensions so well, Berry added, that in battle, signals were nearly unnecessary.[5]

Nelson's impact, therefore, did not end with his death. Not only did his leaders continue his legacy of excellence, but they also continued building other leaders to perpetuate that legacy through generations. Leaders today can follow his example and build a "leadership pipeline." Your most important job as a leader isn't to produce quality products or high profits; it's to produce other leaders. You should constantly be scanning the horizon in search of great talent that can be groomed in positions of leadership. Mentoring other leaders should take a large portion of your time, energy, and focus.

To really gauge the effectiveness of a leader, don't assess his or her performance alone; assess that of the leaders he or she has developed. Good leaders can be identified because their people consistently turn in superior performances. As Larry Bossidy, former CEO of Honeywell and former GE vice-chairman, wrote, "When you're confused about how you're doing as a leader, find out how the people you lead are doing. You'll know the answer."[6] The true mark of a great leader isn't personal performance; it's generational impact through the development of other leaders.

Illustration #2: The Royal Navy's Impact on Shutting Down the Slave Trade

Many of us in the United States view Abraham Lincoln as the leader who caused the abolishment of slavery. The truth is that the United States was one of the last countries to abolish the unconscionable practice and was simply following Britain's lead.

Thanks largely to the efforts of reformers such as William Wilberforce, Zachary Macaulay, and William Pitt, Great Britain abolished the slave trade in 1807, though the practice of slavery would remain for the next two decades. In 1815, the Napoleonic Wars finally ended. Britain was still the world's dominant military force, but now, as it entered a new era of relative peace, its test would be whether it could wield its power for good. Lord Castlereagh, Britain's foreign minister, was fully committed to wiping out the slave trade not only in British territories but across the globe. Britain enjoyed unprecedented command of the seas, and he believed that its power should be used toward that end. (Ironically, the British slave trade had launched the career of the Royal Navy's founder, John Hawkins.) In addition to his efforts at home, at the Congress of Vienna, at which a European peace settlement was created following the Napoleonic Wars, Castlereagh also persuaded France, Holland, Spain, and Portugal to accept abolition. He also got the participating nations to sign an agreement condemning the trade. Furthermore, he set up a Conference of Ambassadors to monitor the signed agreements as well as a series of international admiralty courts to enforce the ban.

By mid-1819, some twenty British ships were stationed in Sierra Leone, patrolling the Atlantic coast of Africa in search of slaving vessels. The British kept a strong presence there over the next *forty years*. This war on the slave trade operated similar to a blockade, but the Royal Navy quickly discovered that large ships of the line were useless in the enterprise and that frigates, schooners, and other small ships were much more suited to the job. Speed and maneuverability were vital. Herman wrote that the captains, commanders, and lieutenants of these vessels "willingly risked their lives for a cause which, whatever their feelings when they started, became a passion, even an obsession, as they experienced the slave trade firsthand."[7]

One young sailor, Thomas Pasley, described boarding a slave vessel:

> In my life I have never witnessed anything so shocking. About 450 people were packed into that small vessel as you would pack bales of goods; and diseases of all sorts became rife with them. One hundred had died before she was taken, and they were and are still dying daily....Some children were in the last stages of emaciation and sores. It was dreadful, and so distressing I could have cried.[8]

The work was acutely frustrating for these passionate souls. They were more likely to die from disease on the mosquito-ridden coast than to be killed in battle. Technical rules hampered their efforts. For example, they could not seize slave ships unless there were actually captives on board. Many slavers often threw their prisoners overboard before the navy could board their ships. Indifferent judges often nullified their efforts by letting captured slavers go. The slavery-tolerating United States refused to allow any of its ships to be searched, which caused every slaving vessel to fly the US flag.

Between 1810 and 1849, the Admiralty freed about 116,000 slaves — compared to the close to one million who got away from their patrols. The volume of the slave traffic actually *increased* during the period. But the British government refused to give up. In 1833, Britain completely abolished slavery in its territories. By the 1840s, the navy had thirty-five vessels committed to the cause on the African coast. Britain also forced other nations to accept an "equipment clause" in the slave trade ban, which meant that the navy could seize ships that carried shackles and other equipment of the trade. The new foreign minister, Lord Palmerston, gave naval officers permission to stop and search any ship flying the US flag, as long as they had good reason to believe that the ship was not actually American. This caused the United States to step up and set up its own anti-slave patrol against its own merchants.

By 1850, the British finally gained momentum in their campaign and eventually succeeded entirely. Herman wrote:

> The end of West Africa's slave trade, the last surviving servant of the old world system, marked the close of one era. The arrival of direct British rule marked the opening of another. For all its setbacks and occasional hypocrisies, the campaign against the slave trade had succeeded, giving the Royal Navy an altruistic humanitarian gloss it never quite lost.[9]

Understanding and Application

Having defeated all of its military enemies, with nothing left to prove, the Royal Navy could have gone into simple maintenance mode. But rather than rest on its laurels, it set its sights on new goals—an obsessive quest, to be more precise. The Royal Navy used its power for good.

Untold millions through generations have benefitted from its enduring legacy.

Great ideas, inspiring vision, noble causes, when communicated and lived with passion from a Level 4 or 5 Leader, take on a life of their own. Small ideas and dull vision wither and fade away. The bigger your vision, the more likely it is to survive beyond you. As Johann Wolfgang von Goethe said, "Dream no small dreams for they have no power to move the hearts of men."[10] What you stand for—as long it's big enough—lives on. The vision and passion of Wilberforce and Castelreagh ignited passion in the hearts of captains and sailors alike. It gave them staying power to push through tremendous obstacles.

Likewise, leaders who want to leave a legacy must inspire a bold and noble vision in the hearts of their people. They must stand for something that attacks the status quo and makes the world a better place. They must be about an elevated cause and not just bottom-line profits.

Summary

The impact of a great leader is seen or felt not only while he or she is living but also long after he or she has passed on. Great leaders are learners and high performers. But they are more than this. They are also great mentors. They develop other leaders. They are passionate visionaries. They see how things are and envision how they can be, and they inspire that vision in the hearts of others. As Orrin Woodward and I wrote in *Launching a Leadership Revolution*:

A Level 5 Leader can be identified by the magnitude of the following he or she leaves behind. The size of the vision, its enduring legacy, and its successful continuation in the hands of other leaders are the fruit of a Level 5 Leader's efforts. Whereas Level 1 Leaders are only as good as what they learn, Level 2 Leaders are only as good as their personal performance, Level 3 Leaders are only as good as the performance of their team, Level 4 Leaders are only as good as the performance of their leaders, and Level 5 Leaders are only as good as the enduring quality and succession of their vision.[11]

Leadership is about far more than what you can accomplish alone. It's about what you can cause to be accomplished with or without your physical presence. Leaders fail when they fail to inspire others. As long as your impact is dependent on you personally digging in the trenches, it will be limited, and it will never perpetuate beyond your personal efforts. Your knowledge, skills, and vision must be duplicated by training and developing other leaders. You can't carry the torch yourself throughout your entire lifetime and then expect others to pick it up after you pass on. It must be passed on while you're alive through mentoring and giving your leaders opportunities to grow and shine.

Great leadership isn't how bright you shine. It's how well you ignite a fire in other people and make them shine.

This is how you make a big difference. This is how you change the world. This is how you leave an enduring legacy.

NOTES

Introduction

1. Tom Holland, *Persian Fire: The First World Empire and the Battle for the West* (New York: Anchor Books, 2007), p. 251.

2. Library of Congress, *Respectfully Quoted: A Dictionary of Quotations: The Essential Reference Guide for Writers and Speechmakers* (Mineola, NY: Dover Publications, 2010), p. 381-382.

3. Barbara W. Tuchman, *The First Salute: A New View of the American Revolution* (New York: Ballantine Books, 1988), p. 124.

4. Adam Nicolson, *Seize the Fire: Heroism, Duty, and Nelson's Battle of Trafalgar* (New York: HarperCollins Publishers, 2005), p. 66.

5. John Lehman, *On Seas of Glory: Heroic Men: Great Ships, and Epic Battles of the American Navy* (New York: The Free Press, 2001), p. 2.

Chapter 1

1. Roy Adkins and Lesley Adkins, *The War for All the Oceans: From Nelson at the Nile to Napoleon at Waterloo* (London: Penguin Books, 2006), p. 2.

2. Ibid., p. 57.

3. Ibid., p. 55.

4. Ibid., p. 58.

5. Ibid., p. 59.

6. Theodore Roosevelt, *Theodore Roosevelt: An Autobiography* (New York: MacMillan, 1913; Digireads. com Publishing, 2011), p. 189.

7. *Wisdom for the Soul: Five Millennia of Prescriptions for Spiritual Healing*, edited by Larry Chang (Washington, DC: Gnosophia Publishers, 2006), p. 391.

8. Lehman, *On Seas of Glory*, p. 66.

9. Ibid.

10. Tuchman, *The First Salute*, p. 241.

11. Michael A. Palmer, *Command at Sea: Naval Command and Control Since the Sixteenth Century* (Cambridge, MA: Harvard University Press, 2005), p. 140.

12. Ibid., p. 224.

13. Ibid., p. 143.

14. Admiral Hood in a letter to Charles Middleton on September 30, 1781, as printed in *Publications of the Navy Records Society, Vol. XXXII, The Barham Papers, Vol. I: Letters and Papers of Charles, Lord Barham, Admiral of the Red Squadron 1758-1813*, edited by Sir John Knox Laughton, M.A., D. Litt. (Great Britain: Navy Records Society, 1907), p. 125.

15. Tuchman, *The First Salute*, p. 245.

16. Ibid., p. 295.

Chapter 2

1. Palmer, *Command at Sea*, p. 178.

2. Ibid.

3. Naval History and Heritage Command, "Biographies in Naval History: Did Jones Actually Say, 'I have not yet begun to fight?'" www.history.navy.mil/bios/jones_jp_did.htm; "'I have not yet begun to fight': The Story of John Paul Jones," www.history.navy.mil/trivia/trivia02a.htm, accessed 10/13/2014.

4. Palmer, *Command at Sea*, p. 188.

5. Nathan Miller, *Broadsides: The Age of Fighting Sail, 1775-1815* (New York: John Wiley & Sons, Inc., 2000), p. 225.

6. Ibid., p. 226.

7. Ibid., p. 227.

8. Ibid., p. 234.

9. Ibid., p. 227.

10. Ibid., p. 228.

11. Adkins and Adkins, *The War for All the Oceans*, p. 86.

12. Palmer, *Command at Sea*, p. 189.

13. Ibid., p. 190.

14. Ibid., p. 190-191.

15. Miller, *Broadsides*, p. 233.

16. Adkins and Adkins, *The War for All the Oceans*, p. 89.

17. Palmer, *Command at Sea*, p. 188.

18. Adkins and Adkins, *The War for All the Oceans*, p. 89.

19. Arthur Herman, *To Rule the Waves: How the British Navy Shaped the Modern World* (London: Hodder and Stoughton, 2004), p. 275-276.

20. Ibid., p. 276.

21. Frank McLynn, *1759: The Year Britain Became Master of the World* (New York: Atlantic Monthly Press, 2004), p. 382.

22. Library of Congress, *Respectfully Quoted*, p. 255.

Chapter 3

1. Herman, *To Rule the Waves*, p. 342.

2. Peter Padfield, *Maritime Supremacy and the Opening of the Western Mind: Naval Campaigns that Shaped the Modern World* (Woodstock, NY: The Overlook Press, Peter Mayer Publishers, 2000), p. 204.

3. Ibid., p. 208-212.

4. Ibid., p. 212.

5. Palmer, *Command at Sea*, p.171.

6. Ibid., p. 175.

7. Captain A. T. (Alfred Thayer) Mahan, D.C.L., LL.D., *The Life of Nelson: The Embodiment of the Sea Power of Great Britain*, Volume I, Second Edition, Revised (Boston: Little, Brown, and Company, 1899), p. 234.

8. Ibid., p. 244.

9. Ibid., p. 253-254.

10. Palmer, *Command at Sea*, p.177.

11. Ibid., p. 177-178.

12. Kevin Kruse, "100 Best Quotes on Leadership," *Forbes*, posted October 16, 2012 at 8:37 a.m., www.forbes.com/sites/kevinkruse/2012/10/16/quotes-on-leadership/.

13. Ian W. Toll, *Six Frigates: The Epic History of the Founding of the U.S. Navy* (New York: W. W. Norton & Company, 2006), p. 405.

14. Theodore Roosevelt, *The Naval War of 1812* (New York: The Knickerbocker Press, 1882), p. 184.

15. Toll, *Six Frigates*, p. 417.

Chapter 4

1. Navy Records Society (Great Britain), *Publications of the Navy Records Society, Volume XI, Papers Relating to the Navy during the Spanish War 1585-1587*, edited by Julian S. Corbett, LL.M., Barrister-At-Law (Great Britain: Navy Records Society, 1898), p. 36.

2. Stephen Coote, *Drake: A Life and Legend of an Elizabethan Hero* (New York: Thomas Dunne Books, 2005), p. 6.

3. Herman, *To Rule the* Waves, p. 114.

4. Colin Martin and Geoffrey Parker, *The Spanish Armada: Revised Edition* (Manchester, UK: Mandolin, Manchester University Press, 1999), p. 131.

5. Jacques Mordal, *25 Centuries of Sea Warfare* (London: Souvenir Press, 1965).

6. Coote, *Drake*, p. 2.

7. Neil Hanson, *The Confident Hope of a Miracle: The True History of the Spanish Armada* (New York: Vintage Books, Random House, 2006), p. 201.

8. Ibid., p. 64.

9. Ibid., p. 65.

10. Ibid., p. 410.

11. Palmer, *Command at Sea*, p. 32.

12. Hanson, *The Confident Hope of a Miracle*, p. 102.

13. Nicolson, *Seize the Fire*, p. 223.

14. Roy Adkins, *Nelson's Trafalgar: The Battle That Changed the World*, (New York: Viking Penguin, 2005), p. 344.

Chapter 5

1. Palmer, *Command at* Sea, p. 65.
2. Ibid., p. 142.
3. Robert B. Kieding, *Scuttlebutt: Tales and Experiences of a Life at Sea* (Bloomington, IN: iUniverse, 2011), p. 175.
4. Donald Thomas, *Cochrane: Britannia's Last Sea-King* (New York: The Viking Press, 1978), p. 65.
5. Ibid., p. 66.
6. Ibid., p. 67.
7. Miller, *Broadsides*, p. 306.

Chapter 6

1. Palmer, *Command at Sea*, p. 144.
2. Ibid., p. 100.
3. Herman, *To Rule the Waves*, p. 356.
4. Ibid., p. 359.

Chapter 7

1. Adkins and Adkins, *The War For All the Oceans*, p. 23.
2. Ibid., p. 24.
3. Ibid., p. 357.
4. Herman, *To Rule the Waves*, p. 357.
5. Miller, *Broadsides*, p. 208.
6. Palmer, *Command at Sea*, p. 158.
7. Ibid., p. 159.

8. Ibid., p. 159.

9. Ibid., p. 160.

10. Ibid., p. 96.

Chapter 8

1. Adkins, *Nelson's Trafalgar*, p. 85.

2. Solar Navigator, "The Battle of Trafalgar 1805," copyright 2006 NJK, www.solarnavigator.net/history/the_battle_of_trafalgar.htm, accessed October 30, 2014.

3. New World Encyclopedia, "Battle of Trafalgar," last modified January 8, 2013 at 16:32, www.newworldencyclopedia.org/entry/Battle_of_Trafalgar, accessed October 30, 2014.

4. Adkins, *Nelson's Trafalgar*, p. 204.

5. David Howarth, *Trafalgar: The Nelson Touch*, Great Battles Series (Gloucestershire, UK: The Windrush Press, 1997), p. 42.

6. Nicolson, *Seize the Fire*, p. 199.

7. Howarth, *Trafalgar: The Nelson Touch*, p. 83.

8. Herman, *To Rule the Waves*, pg. 376.

9. Nicolson, *Seize the Fire*, p. 9-10.

10. Herman, *To Rule the Waves*, pg. 386.

11. Nicolson, *Seize the Fire*, p. 199.

12. Palmer, *Command at Sea*, p. 112.

13. Ibid., p. 122.

14. Montagu Burrows, *The Life of Edward Lord Hawke: Admiral of the Fleet, Vice-Admiral of Great Britain, and First Lord of the Admiralty from 1766 to 1771* (London: W. H. Allen & Co., Limited, 1896), p. 221.

15. Herman, *To Rule the Waves*, p. 288.

16. Ibid., p. 284.

17. Ibid.

18. Ibid., p. 377.

19. Nicolson, *Seize the Fire*, p. 24.

20. Herman, *To Rule the Waves*, p. 333.

21. Ibid., p. 395.

22. Ibid., p. 286.

23. Palmer, *Command at Sea*, p. 91.

24. Herman, *To Rule the Waves*, p. 381.

25. Palmer, *Command at Sea*, p. 12.

26. Ibid., p. 13.

27. Thomas Joseph Pettigrew, F.R.S. F.S.A., *Memoirs of the Life of Vice-Admiral Lord Viscount Nelson, K. B., Duke of Bronté, Volume II* (London: T. and W. Boone, 1869), p. 445.

28. Palmer, *Command at Sea*, p. 179.

29. Herman, *To Rule the Waves*, p. 384.

30. Ibid., p. 449.

Chapter 9

1. Palmer, *Command at Sea*, p. 156.

2. Ibid.

3. Ibid., p. 157.

4. Ibid., p. 156.

5. Ibid., p. 105.

6. Ibid.

7. Ibid., p. 106.

8. Voltaire (François-Marie Arouet), *Candide* (Dover Thrift Edition, 1991), p. 64.

9. Dr. John Campbell, *Naval History of Great Britain: Including the History and Lives of the British Admirals, Volume VIII* (London: Baldwin and Co., 1818), p. 373.

10. Adkins and Adkins, *The War for All the Oceans*, p. 271.

11. Ibid., p. 275.

12. Ibid., p. 276.

13. Ibid., p. 278.

14. Donald Thomas, *Cochrane: Britannia's Sea Wolf* (New York, The Viking Press, 1978), p. 263.

15. Earl of Thomas Barnes Cochrane Dundonald and Henry Richard Fox Bourne, *The Life of Thomas, Lord Cochrane: Tenth Earl of Dundonald, G.C.B., Admiral of the Red, Rear-Admiral of the Fleet* (Middlesex, UK: The Echo Library, 2007), p. 89.

16. Thomas, *Cochrane*, p. 267.

17. Lehman, *On Seas of Glory*, p. 84.

18. Adkins and Adkins, *The War for All the Oceans*, p. 86.

19. Lehman, *On Seas of Glory*, p. 84.

20. Wikimedia Foundation, Inc., "Buck passing," *Wikipedia*, last modified November 2, 2014 at 14:40, accessed on November 3, 2014, en.wikipedia.org/wiki/Buck_passing.

Chapter 10

1. Palmer, *Command at Sea*, p. 319-320.

2. Ibid., p. 320.

3. J.D. Steinbruner, *The Cybernetic Theory of Decision: New Dimensions of Political Analysis* (Princeton, NJ: Princeton University Press, 1973), p. 16.

4. Palmer, *Command at Sea*, p. 321.

5. Tuchman, *The First Salute*, p. 125.

6. Carl von Clausewitz, *On War*, edited and translated by Michael Howard and Peter Paret (Princeton, NJ: Princeton University Press, 1989), p. 117-121.

7. Herman, *To Rule the Waves*, p. 347.

8. Vicki Singleton, "The Battle of Cape St. Vincent," *Chasing Nelson*, copyright © 2013 Vicki Singleton, www.admiralnelson.info/CapeStVincent4.html, accessed November 3, 2014.

Chapter 11

1. Herman, *To Rule the Waves*, p. 395.

2. Ibid., p. 399.

3. Ibid., p. 401.

4. Chris Brady and Orrin Woodward, *Launching a Leadership Revolution: Mastering the Five Levels of Influence* (Flint, MI: Obstaclés Press, 2012), p. 203.

5. Miller, *Broadsides*, p. 201.

6. J. Stewart Black and Hal Gregersen, *Leading Strategic Change: Breaking through the Brain Barrier* (Upper Saddle River, NJ: Financial Times Prentice Hall, 2003), p. 136.

7. Herman, *To Rule the Waves*, p. 421.

8. Ibid.

9. Ibid., p. 423.

10. Christopher Howse, "Gordon Brown Improves Goethe's Line," The Telegraph, last updated September 29, 2014, copyright © 2014 Telegraph Media Group Limited, http://blogs.telegraph.co.uk/culture/christopherhowse/100003609/gordon-brown-improves-goethes-line/, accessed November 3, 2014.

11. Brady and Woodward, *Launching a Leadership Revolution*, p. 238-239.

ACKNOWLEDGMENTS

Sometimes I think books should be more like movies. Instead of one name on the cover, there ought to be a roll of credits at the end. In that regard, may the reader now envision the names and titles below making their way up a silver screen. And to add drama that is appropriate to the theme of this book, let's mix in some tumultuous waves and victorious action music. Now stay seated and finish off that final popcorn as I thank the following awesome people for helping to make this book a reality:

Jim and Gayle Brady: Ideal Parents
Terri Brady: Heroine
Casey, Nathaniel, Christine, and JR: Star Cast
Orrin and Laurie Woodward: Executive Business Partners
Rob Hallstrand: Executive Director
Norm Williams: Graphic Designer
Doug Huber: Assistant to the Author
Tracey Avereyn: Social Networker Extraordinaire
Michelle Turner: Director
Deborah Brady (no relation): Editor
Bill Rousseau: Production Manager
Ryan Renz: Media Manager
Leading Characters:
    Tim and Amy Marks
    Claude and Lana Hamilton
    George and Jill Guzzardo
    Bill Lewis
    Dan and Lisa Hawkins
Stephen Palmer: Screenplay Writer

And finally: may all honor and glory go to my Lord and Savior Jesus Christ.

Other Books by Chris Brady

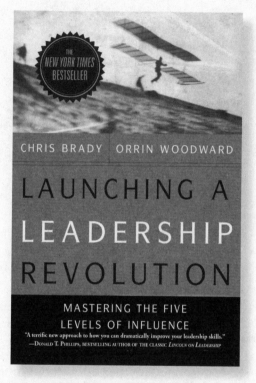

Launching a Leadership Revolution: Mastering the Five Levels of Influence **by Chris Brady and Orrin Woodward – $15.95**
This *New York Times* bestseller demonstrates how the principles of leadership apply to anyone and everyone. The question isn't whether you are a leader but, rather, will you be ready when you're called upon to lead? Let Orrin and Chris teach you the art and science of leadership, so you'll be ready when the spotlight shines on you!
This product is also available as an audio book for $29.95.

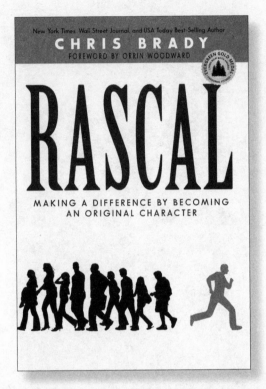

Rascal: Making a Difference by Becoming an Original Character **by Chris Brady with Foreword by Orrin Woodward – $21.95**

Rascal won the Personal Growth Gold Medal in the 2013 Living Now Evergreen Book Awards. Discover how to develop the character of a Rascal, to get out of line and be different in order to make a difference. Your individual future and the future of freedom depend on it. Get in touch with your Rascalinity and use it to break barriers and catapult you ahead of your peers. Live your life on purpose for a purpose and make your own unique contribution to the world!

This product is also available as an audio book for $29.95.

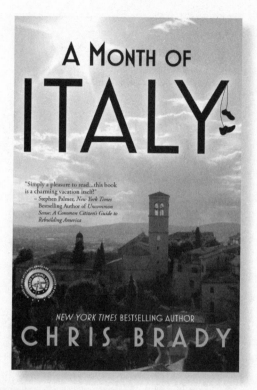

A Month of Italy: Rediscovering the Art of Vacation by Chris Brady – $15.95

A Month of Italy won a 2013 Gold ADDY Award for its cover design and is featured in the major motion picture *A Long Way Off*. This story is one of going slow in order to go fast; it's about rediscovering and bringing back a lost art, namely the art of vacation, and it is—or rather should be—a story about you. With wit and wisdom, Chris details the adventures of the Brady family's month-long sabbatical in picturesque Italy. Kick back and relax with your copy today and be inspired to take your own "radical sabbatical"!

This product is also available as an audio book for $29.95.

PAiLS: 20 Years from Now, What Will You Wish You Had Done Today? by Chris Brady – $19.95

"Your place in this world is an address only you can occupy."
Chris Brady provides a fresh approach to finding meaning as he
leads you through the adventure of your life like a veteran tour
guide. Learn how to determine a clear direction toward living
the life you've always wanted. Discover today how to give your
unique best, live your most satisfying and rewarding life, and
leave a worthwhile and beneficial legacy—because the world is
waiting for the important contribution that only you can make!
This product is also available as an audio book for $19.95.